ORDINARY DAYS and TENDER PLACES

ORDINARY DAYS and TENDER PLACES

HOW WE TALK (AND DON'T TALK) ABOUT ADOPTION

MARGARET BENDROTH

BEACON PRESS, BOSTON

Beacon Press
24 Farnsworth Street
Boston, Massachusetts
www.beacon.org

Beacon Press books
are published under the auspices of
the Unitarian Universalist Association of Congregations.

Printed in the United States of America

29 28 27 26 8 7 6 5 4 3 2 1

This book is printed on acid-free paper that meets the uncoated paper ANSI/NISO specifications for permanence as revised in 1992.

Text design by BookMatters, Berkeley

Library of Congress Cataloguing-in-Publication Data
is available for this title.
Hardcover ISBN: 978-0-8070-2510-9
E-book ISBN: 978-0-8070-2511-6
Audiobook: 978-0-8070-2600-7

The authorized representative in the EU for product safety and compliance is Easy Access System Europe 16879218, Mustamäe tee 50, 10621 Tallinn, Estonia: https://beacon.org/eu-contact.

CONTENTS

INTRODUCTION

Adoptions are rare in American society. Right now only about 2 to 4 percent of Americans have adopted a child, or, to put it another way, adoptees account for less than 1.5 percent of the US population, some 5 million out of 350 million—and no wonder. Just listen to the way we talk about them. I have been asked if I am my children's "real mother," as if ours is an artificial, perhaps even unnatural, family of last resort. "No offense," someone says to my daughter, "but what's it like to be adopted?" The question may be well intentioned, but it is also unanswerable. There is, after all, no way to prove you are not marked or defective, stuck in a jury-rigged life, the arbitrary child of utter strangers.[1]

There are so many stories out there, after all, alarming accounts of botched placements, exploited birth parents, and wounded children. Who could forget Baby Jessica, the two-year-old returned by the court system to birth parents who had belatedly changed their minds? Or the "child catchers" prowling Central America, bundling babies off to unsuspecting white American homes? We read of birth parents enduring lifelong grief and loss, and adoptees suffering emotional damage that can lead to mental illness, addiction, and even suicide. *Adopted child syndrome*, as it has been called, is a daunting hodgepodge of psychological problems, from attachment disorders and anxieties to downright deviant behaviors, eating disorders, alcohol and drug abuse, even an "inclination towards crime."[2]

The defenders of adoption have another set of stories, however. They point out, rightly, that our present-day practices are far different from the old system, built as it was on secrecy and shame. Not all that long ago, adoptees were legally denied from even seeing their original birth certificates. The majority of adoptions today are open, meaning that they involve two sets of parents who are known to each other and to the child they share. Defenders of adoption can also point to plenty of success stories: famous, well-adjusted, and accomplished adoptees such as Steve Jobs and NFL quarterback Colin Kaepernick, musicians and television stars such as Faith Hill and Melissa Gilbert. This seems powerful proof that love has the power to overcome every point of difference, whether it is racial prejudice, culture, or physical disability. It's no accident that if you google the word *adoption*, the result is a deluge of images of enthusiastically grateful dogs and cats "rescued" from high-kill shelters. There's a part of us that wants to believe that the bottom line is altruism.

Yet somehow all the stories in the world don't seem to dispel our unease. After the US Supreme Court overturned the *Roe v. Wade* decision in 2022, effectively allowing states to outlaw abortion, many people expected the number of adoptions to grow accordingly. But they haven't. As far as we can tell at this point, over 90 percent of the women who are denied abortions will end up raising their children or turning to the foster care system; only about 9 percent will choose to relinquish them. The reasons are complicated—and we will explore many of them in the pages ahead—but clearly the statistics tell an important story. Beyond the standard parameters of our contemporary debates, our unending standoff about the rights of the unborn versus a woman's right to choose, there are the thousands upon thousands of children for whom we are now—and have always been—responsible.[3]

We are uneasy. Adoption just seems risky, perhaps even a recipe for trouble. Even the best-intentioned adoptive parents are playing with fire, warns Gabrielle Glaser in a recent critique of the "secret history of adoption." In the end, it is a permanent "loss for the adoptee." No matter how strong or consistent, love will never be enough.[4]

Across the wide span of human experience, however, that's a pretty narrow view. Adoption is, after all, an age-old practice, one of the many ways people have formed family ties and cared for the vulnerable. We find it in the Babylonian code of Hammurabi and the laws of China, Greece, and ancient Rome. Raising other people's children is still an accepted way of life in many cultures around the world. "There are societies," writes anthropologist Fiona Bowie, "in which adoption is not only common, but an essential and often preferred means of raising children." Non-biological parenthood is not "stigmatized second-best," in these cultures but instead is "ubiquitous."[5]

Even in modern American society there are "other mothers" and kinship networks, godparents and aunties, multigenerational households and families created by choice rather than biology. Ellen Herman, one of the foremost historians of American adoption, poses the question starkly: "When, how, and why did the exchange of children—an ancient transaction traditionally tied to concerns about property and charity—become a process requiring intensive scrutiny, information management, psychological sensitivity, and instruction and guidance by professionals?"[6]

Or, to put it another way, why do we worry so?

I write as an adoptive mother, now with two grown children and a small nest of adorable grandchildren—and that means I do not take any of these concerns lightly. I understand the hesitation. I know through my own experience that adoption is not a simple solution, certainly not an easy fix to childlessness. My children have struggled with big unanswerable questions about identity and belonging, and I know that they live with losses that my husband and I cannot erase. And though I have never been pregnant, I can see, as anyone can, that there is no emotionally simple way to carry a child for nine months, go through the ordeal of birth, and then place your infant in the hands of a stranger.

Nor do I present my experience as any kind of standard. We adopted our children as infants through a private agency; now somewhere around half of placements are from public agencies and foster care. Today the typical adoptee is older—in 2021 the average age was six, and a third of the total number of adoptees were nine or older—and the adoptive parents are far more diverse. Many are relatives, stepparents, or single women, and now, after many hard-fought legal battles, same-sex couples. LGBTQ families, in fact, are four times more likely than their heterosexual counterparts to be built by adoption.[7] So I am well aware that many of the people reading this book, whether from adoptive families or otherwise, may not identify with the stories I tell. But that's not the point, really.

I am also writing as a historian, as someone who, by training and inclination, takes the long view. Studying the past has widened my perspective on the present, challenged my assumptions about what we consider normal and proper. It tells me that much of our worry is circumstantial, specific to our time and place. Many of our concerns about adoption are, in other words, artifacts of twenty-first-century life. Without a doubt, there's plenty to be concerned about these days, with so many of our established beliefs in flux. We are questioning so much—the rules and reasons for family life, the meaning of motherhood, and the proper care of children. And so I'm going to suggest that our discomfort with adoption owes much to big and well-warranted concerns about our fraying human ties, widespread loneliness and isolation, and our distrust of institutions and of each other.

The backstory to our present-day anxiety about adoption is long and complicated, but as I aim to show in this book, it goes a long way to explain both our negativity and our idealism. There are circumstantial reasons for our confused and contradictory fears about our children, how we are at once so obsessed with their welfare and willing to tolerate inexcusable rates of child poverty. There are historical, not necessarily scientific, reasons behind the widespread assumption that biological blood ties are superior to all the rest, why we assume that families without a clear line of genetic inheritance are compromised from the start.

The fact is, adoption touches us in tender places. It poses painful questions about selfhood, what it means to be an "authentic" person in an age driven by algorithms and artificiality. The adopted child's questions about the self and personhood are ours as well, though perhaps more focused and more urgent. Their wonderings about what is determined by fate and what is chosen remind us of the unanswerable dilemmas we all face as we navigate the narrow spaces between free will and determinism. Is it surprising, in a time when loneliness has become epidemic, that so much of our talk about adoption is about separation and trauma? In our more honest moments, we know that we are all at risk.

Adoption is not easy. It calls into question our entire social order, our tolerance of economic inequality, and our bland assurances to the poor. It is not a "private matter," writes sociologist Christine Ward Gailey, for it "involves people with different degrees of social power in a society of ever-increasing wealth differences, racial and ethnic hierarchies, and uneven but persistent discrimination by gender and sexual orientation."[8] No wonder many people find it a deeply ambivalent experience. "Someday," one adoptive mother writes, "I will explain to my children that I love them enough to wish I had never met them. Even though they bring me intense joy, I would gladly give up every bit of that happiness if that sacrifice meant they were born into a family that could love and care for them the way all children deserve to be loved and cared for."[9]

All of these open questions have made the age-old practice of adoption a problem. They have created both unrealistic expectations and outsized worries, well-meant but painful questions about whether a nongenetic family like mine has a chance to be mentally and spiritually whole. Though I cannot (and will not) propose specific ways in which the world must be changed or, mercifully, offer parenting advice, I can tell my own story about what it's like to create, build, and keep a family together without the supportive ties of biological kinship.

Though this is not a personal memoir, the chapters of this book loosely follow my own life, my experiences with childlessness, then wanting children, and finally spending years learning to love them deeply and well. It dives into questions about what holds families together, the mysteries of genetic inheritance, and the long-term effects of trauma. I draw from my own historical understanding as well as what I've gleaned from experts in fields different from my own—evolutionary biology, anthropology, philosophy, even a little theology now and then. But in the end, much of this book consists of the musings of a twenty-first-century woman well into her sixties, neither young nor very old, still trying to figure out what really matters, what constitutes success in parenting—or in life.

Though my children and husband appear in these pages from time to time, I include their stories carefully. Like a lot of adoptees, Nathan and Anna have already spent far too much time explaining themselves to strangers. This is not their book, I know for a fact. Nor is it necessarily the way they would reconstruct things, but, I would add, it is true nonetheless. I've tried to ease their burden by including other stories, especially those of other adoptees. It's a literature with considerable depth and range, coming from wise and compassionate people. The message, as you will see, is not easy, but it's important.

I offer my story not as some shining example or a morality tale for others to benefit by—after all, it's ongoing and far from settled. But I am guessing that other people share my questions, including adoptive parents, adopted children, and really anyone who suspects that what we consider normal is not necessarily a good thing. "If you step just an inch off 'ordinary' family—the inch that adoption moves you," writes sociologist and adoptive parent Barbara Katz Rothman, "...you get a fresh angle on family."[10] Like a sudden glance into a mirror, when you are confronted with the truth of your appearance, listening to adoptive families reveals what we far too often take for granted. My guess is that my particular frustrations and challenges are not unique; we are all wondering how to navigate a need to belong in a world that seems hell-bent on pulling us apart.

I also write as a person of faith, albeit one with lots of questions and uncertain loyalties. So don't worry. If my religious experiences have given me anything, it is a particular sensitivity to tragedy, an instant skepticism toward easy nostrums and pat reassurances. My childhood church emphasized rigor; as a child I absorbed some stark and difficult teachings about God's will and human inability, and these have stayed with me—despite all my efforts to look in other directions. At its worst, my religion has made me critical and snarky; at best, it has pushed me to take up hard things, in fact many of the kinds of questions behind this book, about failure and success, belonging and separateness.

Ultimately, this is a book about differences. I have heard, over and over, the well-meaning insistence that my two adopted children are "no different" from their biologically related cousins, that in every meaningful way we are just the same. And I have often insisted that my family is not damaged or defective; we are normal parents and children, living together just as if we had met in a maternity ward instead of the waiting room of an adoption agency. In a lot of ways, that's true. Our daily lives, like those of countless others, have mostly consisted of jobs and school and friends.

But we are also very, very different.

That's surprisingly hard to say. No adopted child, after all, wants to be reminded regularly that they are the product of painful circumstances, nor do their parents. Our social instinct is to be supportive, recognizing that adoptive families need to be mainstreamed, not called out or stigmatized.

But sometimes the differences matter, and not just to people like me. We all need adoptive families, with all their pain and problems, now maybe more than ever. Families like mine are, by definition, not shiny or frictionless, the kind we hold out as an ideal. They are formed when someone has to say goodbye, whether to an infant, a dream of biological children, or a perfect life of happy harmony. In every instance, there is a need for honesty and forgiveness, a love that goes down to the depths, that can weather anger, sorrow, and unanswerable loss.

Adoptive families, regardless of how they came to be together, the number of parents involved, or their race or gender or sexuality, are important for everyone. I would hazard a guess that every home, not just adoptive ones, sees its share of pain and disappointment. Marriages sputter, children grow resentful, bills and disease and expensive house repairs breed despair. No one measures up to the ideal—and no one benefits from it either. Biological families, however, can maintain the fiction that all is well, especially when the house is clean and the children are college-bound. Adoptive ones cannot. When my husband and I walk down the street with our children, none of us even remotely resembling the other, our private pain is clearly visible. But so is our decision to move beyond it, to make an unconventional family and find our way through the challenges. Every family has its own share of "what happened?" questions—ours simply happen to be out in public. Which is, I believe, a good thing for all of us.

CHAPTER I

CHILDLESS

We begin in a difficult place. Despite all of the blindingly personal issues open for full and frank discussion today, from arcane sexual practices to messy digestive disorders, whether or not you are a parent is still a delicate subject. And it's not hard to see why. These days the simple question, "Do you have children?" might end up in an emotional minefield, including a story of devastating loss, a failed relationship, or, in the face of climate catastrophe, an adamant political position.

But we keep asking, perhaps holding our breath as we wait for the answer. We don't wonder why someone decided to start a family—we want to know why they did not.

After all, parenthood is a primary passageway into adulthood, a genuinely grown-up activity, like taking out a mortgage or paying off college loans. It suggests (even if it isn't true) that you are trustworthy and stable. Having a child means you are a full-fledged member of your local community, the kind of person who cares about schools and playgrounds and neighborhood safety. It comes with the suggestion of unselfishness and maturity: You have clearly managed to make an important life decision and stick with the consequences.

That's all a bit silly, of course. The biology of conception and childbirth have nothing to do with your bank account or your emotional stability—and it's no secret that having children will directly challenge both. There is no direct line between having a baby and being a good citizen. What's more, we don't even award the maturity points evenly: Some people actually lose a few by becoming parents. Society would prefer the poor or chronically unemployed to be childless and remain that way. This silly equation exposes the sneaky moral calculus that has shaped our attitudes toward parenthood, and even more so, the lack of same.

This is, in other words, the complicated place where we begin thinking about adoption. We start by considering that murky "before time," and the way it so often places adoptive families behind the starting line, burdened by doubts about, well, their normality.

A lot of what follows is about infertility and the long history behind the ways we have come to understand and treat it. Some people may find that as interesting as I do; others may consider skipping ahead. I can't really blame you—it's all pretty depressing. I'm also well aware that today many, if not most, adoptive families do not begin with a story like mine. The parents are more likely to be single or a relative, a stepfather or stepmother. They may be people for whom pregnancy is simply not an option, such as disabled adults, men in same-sex relationships, or even someone who, for all kinds of reasons, hasn't ended up with a life partner.

I still think this is a good place to begin. Infertility is more than just a particular kind of physical problem—it's a big and complex metaphor for the painful experience of missing out, of being relegated to the outside through no choice of your own. It's one of many instances when your life veers off a clearly defined path and you find yourself violating the usual markers for success. It's the kind of disappointment for which, more often than not, we never arrive at an explanation—as we'll see, most couples who have difficulty conceiving a child will never receive a clear diagnosis, much less a cure. We want to believe that hard experiences will end with some kind of reward, that Cinderella will find her prince and, as a bonus, become a better, happier person. But sometimes there is no resolution.

That's not necessarily the last word though. As Episcopal theologian Barbara Brown Taylor writes, the quick fix might not be the best one, especially if your goal is to be a thoughtful and compassionate human being. "After years of being taught that the way to deal with painful emotions is to get rid of them," she says, "it can take a lot of reschooling to learn to sit with them instead, finding out from those who feel them what they have learned by sleeping in the wilderness that those who sleep in comfortable houses may never know."[1]

It is not without trepidation, then, that I begin the discussion with my body. More specifically, the center of my lower abdomen, the place where once a month a woman feels that slight twinge, a brief cramp and then a letting go, the signal that her period is coming. I imagine that this is the same place where she begins to suspect something momentous, a new life forming within her. But I would not know—I have never been pregnant.

That's not for want of trying. Back in the 1980s, when I was in graduate school, all the chatter was about a woman's biological imperative, the demand issuing forth from her soul that she must, absolutely must, have a baby. I thought I was experiencing this phenomenon when one day out of the blue I cried over an advertisement for baby food. One moment I was killing time, leafing through a magazine, and the next I was seized by a tangle of emotions I did not even know I had.

In retrospect, none of this is surprising. I was a prime target, a healthy woman in my mid-twenties, assuming without any particular urgency that one day I and my husband would have a family. It helped that I was also unhappy with my life as it was unfolding, a graduate student realizing the futility of 1980s-style academia, with its postmodern this and that, all the competition and the posturing. And so I gave in without much of a struggle. One winter afternoon, as I sat on my couch sobbing over the Gerber baby, I decided to become a mother.

Yes, there were a few logistics to consider. My husband was gobsmacked when I made my announcement, and in that respect I suppose he was no different from the average man who thinks about parenthood with a different kind of urgency. But he was, and is, a kind and empathetic man. Without even a glance at the baby-food advertisement, he agreed to become a father—or perhaps, ever the pragmatic New Englander, he realized it was best not to argue. (Neither of us are good planners, that much should be clear.)

Then there was my own situation. I was three-quarters of the way through graduate school, slogging toward a PhD in American history with uncertain job prospects ahead. I shrugged off all kinds of misgivings about my academic choices, blithely bracketing the stern admonition I'd once received from a woman who had hired me to babysit her three demanding children. Knowing my academic ambitions, she had marched me to a storage closet in her basement and showed me stacks of boxes, research toward a PhD in Russian literature she would never receive. "Look," she said, "and consider yourself warned." Somehow I believed my experience would be different.

It's been said that if you do not know, as a cold hard fact, that you were an idiot in your twenties, then you probably still are one. As it turned out, I had some hard growing up to do. Over the next few years, some unknown combination of God and the universe, my body and my husband's body made hash of my biological imperative. To this day, I can't tell you what went wrong. Round after round of cruel and embarrassing procedures, intrusive tests, and diagnostic surgeries all proved inconclusive. We never received an explanation of the problem, much less a remedy that was not expensive, invasive, and emotionally exhausting.

After a while I gave up wondering. It would happen when it happened. In the meantime, that twinge in my lower abdomen turned into a taunt with a spiteful habit of intruding at the worst time: halfway up a mountain in the Adirondacks or during a plane's final approach into the Nairobi airport. Once it held off for almost a week past its scheduled arrival, giving me several days of cautious joy, only to revert back to form as I was walking to the library for yet another day of dissertation research. A taunt or a sober voice of responsibility, either way the message was clear: *Stay on task, woman.*

THE B-WORD

We no longer use the word *barren* to describe women with my condition, and for good reason. Just type the word into Google and watch the images that come up: bleak stretches of empty land, a desiccated landscape of whitened skeletons and lonely tumbleweeds. Even worse than the physical description, though, is the moral and psychological connotation. According to the *Oxford English Dictionary*, *barren* denotes emptiness, as in "bare of intellectual wealth, destitute of attraction or interest, poor, meagre, jejune, arid, and dry." It can also mean "unproductive, fruitless, and unprofitable" or "unresponsive, dull, yielding no mental fruit." In Japanese and Korean, a barren female is a "woman made of stone."[2]

No wonder that we have substituted a more clinical vocabulary. The Victorians spoke of *sterility*, a medical condition thought to be correctable, though as we will see, their remedies were not for the fainthearted. The twentieth century gave us *infertility*, reflecting a growing scientific awareness that barrenness was a dual affliction, perhaps the woman's problem, perhaps the man's, and perhaps the couple's. Beyond that, the options are thin. A word like *childless* brings at least the suggestion of pain and pity, certainly better than describing oneself as *child-free*, as if cured of an infestation or some burden imposed by invisible others.

The new terminology, medicalized and no doubt designed to be helpful, misses something essential about an empty womb. *Barren*, that stark and antiquated word, speaks to a long, painful, and complex human experience. Medical problems can be corrected or dealt with; we can adapt to childless or child-free lifestyles. But barrenness—in all of its possible manifestations—seeps into the soul. The ancestors were right to give it a spiritual meaning, to evoke deserts and dry bones and vast stretches of emptiness.

Infertility is an odd kind of loss. There is no one to mourn, no one to remember, only an absence. There are no memories, no stories about Grandpa's silly jokes or the foibles of eccentric Aunt Susan, the kind of reminiscing that brings healing. What was lost was never owned in the first place. For a long time, I told myself that this part of my story ended when we adopted Nathan and Anna, that we had found a way to take care of the problem and move on. However, the truth is that there is no simple fix, no instant emotional turnaround triggered by a baby-food advertisement. The loss stays. It nudges and pokes and pinches, in different ways at different times.

The inability to conceive a biological child changes you. It can make you more skeptical about everything, turn you into an outsider, albeit one who for the most part looks and acts like everyone else. "I felt like a miserable, ragged beggar cowering on the fringes of a king's feast," one woman told an infertility researcher. This kind of alienation is powerful enough to turn into loathing: Another research subject declared that she "detest[ed] all pregnant women. They carry their pregnancy like a badge of honor," she said, "when they did nothing special to achieve it. Honestly, they make me sick."[3]

I have certainly gone there. I have been closed off, clinging to bitterness about the unfairness of it all, the ditzy couples conceiving ditzy offspring, one after the other. I have not returned full circle after adopting my children; I am still a woman who has never experienced pregnancy and birth. I will always be a survivor of loss.

But knowing the historical backstory has helped. It has explained to me, in all its dubious glory, the role played by scientific experts and medical professionals in trying to "fix" both infertility and infertile couples. There are big, important reasons why it is so difficult to remove the moral calculus from childlessness and parenthood. The story goes a long, long way back.

YOUR ATTITUDE PROBLEM

We start then, with the way modern Americans talk—or do not talk—about infertility. Like so many other couples struggling to conceive, we received reams of unsolicited, medically questionable advice. "Just relax," we were told, "and you'll get pregnant." Everyone, it seemed, had an anecdote about a friend of a friend of a friend who had a bit of trouble in the beginning but somehow magically destressed and ended up with children hanging from the rafters. And at least half of these parents, it seemed, were in the middle of adoption proceedings when it all happened. No one pointed out how improbable it is that filling out forms and sitting through interviews with social workers helps prospective parents unwind, get sexy, and conceive a child. Never mind that creepy tips about your sex life do not induce relaxation and that stress has never been an effective means of birth control.

Somehow the belief persists that infertility is an attitude problem. It is true, of course, that mind and body are not separate trains running along parallel tracks. Undeniably, our mental and physical health are deeply, mysteriously intertwined. Moreover, we have all heard the warnings that stress weakens the body's defense against disease. We've heard the admonition that serenity is key to a long and healthy life. As a frequent—though never consistent—practitioner of meditation and mindfulness, I have to agree. I know somewhere deep in my bones that a clear, open, and reflective mind is good for me in all kinds of ways.

Still, no one tells someone with a broken arm to take a long soak in the tub or a patient with kidney disease to plan a quiet weekend in the Poconos. We send them directly to a doctor to get the problem taken care of.

Infertility is a complicated situation. In our case, there was no doctor in the picture for months—the rule of thumb is seeking medical help only after a year of trying—and in the meantime, we endured a stream of pseudo-psychological advice, with a few personal anecdotes thrown in for good measure. Over time, the absence of a baby becomes a kind of personal failure.

In that sense, it's not entirely different from the way we think about other illnesses. Everyone feels bad for the victim of lung cancer, but they also wonder why they didn't do the right thing and throw away the cigarettes. Our compassion is laced with a quiet suspicion that chain-smoking Uncle Louie actually willed his untimely end.

The inability to conceive a child is especially shameful though. We have become disconcertingly comfortable talking about all kinds of embarrassing health problems. No one bats an eye over commercials with senior citizens strutting around in adult diapers or a hapless sufferer running off, without explanation, in search of an emergency bathroom. Yet involuntary childlessness remains an intensely private condition, one almost too fraught to describe, even to close friends.

Certainly, one big part of the problem is that it is female. That means that, for thousands of years, infertility has been theorized about and treated by people who did not get pregnant—men. But that's not the main issue. Alongside the garden-variety sexism are centuries of moral history, a deeply rooted, perhaps ineradicable assumption that a childless woman has no one to blame but herself. Even today, our medical terminology is judgmental, with its talk of "incompetent cervixes," "hostile mucus," and "failure to conceive." There are deep historical reasons why infertility is the worst thing that can happen to a woman—and why it is somehow all her fault.

ORIGIN STORIES

In one respect, the problem is obvious. Before microscopes and laboratories, all explanations of fertility and infertility were—and had to be—guesswork. In fact, there was no automatic connection between the act of copulation and a baby. After all, they took place many months apart, perhaps long after the memories, good or bad, had faded.

But what if no baby ever came? For much of Western history, two explanations circulated. The first, the *semence* theory, held that women and men contributed equally to conception. Each emitted a "seed," which, when combined, resulted in pregnancy. The interesting proviso was that in order to conceive, a woman had to experience orgasm. The mechanical explanation was that this created a necessary suction, planting the male seed in the womb. And though this requirement was no doubt a lovely advantage for ancient women, it had a downside: A barren woman was obviously frigid. The "languishing" of a woman's "venereal appetite" doomed her to barrenness; her childlessness was both a painful plight and a sure sign that she was bad in bed.[4]

Aristotle had another theory about females, and it was hardly better. In his view, women were primarily a receptacle for the masculine seed; menstrual blood provided the "form" of the fetus, while the sperm supplied the basic information for creating a new human. Woman's contribution was inert matter, and man's was the force to bring a new life into being. In fact, Aristotle believed that semen was composed of human beings in miniature—he called them *animalcules*—who required only a warm, moist womb in order to grow. There was no question, in other words, about the culprit behind a childless marriage.

Yet in Aristotle's time, the problem reportedly went beyond sexual frigidity: A barren woman was fundamentally off-kilter, both disordered and unstable. Medical theory of the day looked to a balance of essential fluids, or humors, each with separate properties. Blood was warm and moist, phlegm cold and moist; yellow bile was warm and dry, and black bile cold and dry. An infertile woman therefore was unbalanced to her core, either too dry or too wet for those tiny animalcules to take root and flourish. Without too much of a stretch, we can identify the historical roots of modern body-shaming.

Both theories make a certain logical sense—but only as long as women's reproductive organs remain out of sight, shrouded in mystery. Actual discoveries would not happen for centuries, after scientists had all but exhausted the patience of the animal kingdom and begun to explore the inner workings of the human body.

Meanwhile, the Greek belief system persisted. In fact, one of the most popular medical advice books in colonial North America was entitled *Aristotle's Master Piece*. It offered lengthy discourses on the relative humidity and temperature of women's bodies. One of the reigning experts among seventeenth-century midwives, Nicholas Culpeper, explained that conception required sex to be "hot," full of "Spirits, and well tempered." Failure to conceive was due to an "impotency of the womb," an "evil conformation of the privities," or an imbalance of moisture and temperature. A seed might be "choaked in marsh ground" (the woman was fat and damp) or "burned in dry and sandy ground" (she was too skinny and dehydrated). "Hence we may gather," declared Culpeper, echoing Aristotle, "that barrenness is oftener from a fault in the woman than the man, for in men there is nothing required but fruitful seed spent into a fruitful womb."

Aha. Here, it seems, is the source of all that strange nonscientific advice about relaxation. It is a little gratifying that we were spared the rest of Culpeper's advice, most of it more magic than science. Childless women were prescribed a dose of rocket seed, silermontane, and ivory shavings, perhaps with some cinnamon and nutmeg. They might also try sweet almonds, pistachios, hazelnuts, and pine nuts. Moreover, the right kind of bath could help: Culpeper and his colleagues suggested a relaxing soak in a tub sprinkled with alum, niter, and bitumen. Even better, a woman should follow it up by placing a bag of balm on her stomach, preferably filled with calamint, motherwort, and wine. In the end, however, attitude was all; the infertile woman's best friend was a positive approach to life. "A natural bad disposition that causeth barrenness," said Culpeper, "is not curable."[5]

Depressingly, the first medical advances of the late nineteenth and early twentieth centuries maintained the ancient assumption that infertility was a woman's problem. Unless a husband was demonstrably impotent, he was not the cause but the victim of his wife's inability to conceive. We know now that a nightmare epidemic of gonorrhea was a likely cause of infertility during that period—a study of male hospital patients in early twentieth-century Boston, for example, found a third of them infected—but back then, most doctors operated under the policy don't ask, don't tell. The average woman seeking treatment for childlessness went to her doctor's office alone.[6]

American doctors had their first glimpse of female reproductive organs courtesy of French doctors, men who were neither prudish about the female body nor squeamish about autopsies. But the firsthand inspection did not necessarily lead to new insights. The reigning American authority, Augustus Gardner, wrote a major treatise, *On the Causes and Curative Treatment of Sterility, with a Preliminary Statement on the Physiology of Generation* (1856), that essentially upgraded old notions about female fertility. Convinced of a scientific connection between the ovaries and the digestive system, Gardner advised that a "balanced" diet and regular exercise were essential to bearing children. He then discarded perhaps the only theory that women of the past had found beneficial, concluding that orgasm was not necessary for conception. In fact, this eminently proper Victorian declared, conceiving a child was fundamentally a "chemical or mechanical process that was neither enhanced nor inhibited by a woman's sexual pleasure."[7]

Though the diagnoses and the cures were dubious at best, that did not seem to matter. Any path to motherhood was well worth the trouble. This was, after all, the era of "home, sweet home," when the house became a sanctuary and mom became a saint. No longer just the drudge who changed diapers and made dinner, she was a special being endowed with uniquely feminine gifts, all of which combined to make her a perfectly contented caregiver. Motherhood, in other words, was every woman's truest and happiest destiny. And there were no words too emotionally overwrought to describe it. "What a sacred shrine on earth is a fond mother's love," a sentimental Methodist wrote in 1850. "How pure—how unchanging—how deathless!—love as pure as the sunny light of heaven, and as unchanging as the laws that govern the universe."[8]

So what to fix in the childless woman, and how? All kinds of ailments, as it turned out, were amenable to the surgeon's knife. Led by J. Marion Sims, the "father" of gynecology, doctors poked and bored and cut away at obstructive cervixes (often, we should add, without sterilization or anesthesia). The names of the various tools and treatments should have warned off the squeamish: Recamier's curette and the Sims speculum, the hysterotome, uterine guillotine, and uterine injector. Other enthusiasts took to removing ovaries, assuming that all "female diseases," no matter what the symptoms, originated in the reproductive system. All this, while medicine had only the vaguest understanding of how that system actually worked, having never witnessed conception and possessing only a passing knowledge of ovulation. In fact, nineteenth-century medicine had the menstrual cycle exactly wrong: Since females in many other animal species are fertile during estrus, scientists assumed that humans are too. Thus, couples who wanted to avoid pregnancy were advised to restrict sex to the middle of a woman's cycle—but that happens to be when pregnancy is actually most likely.

MORE BODY-SHAMING

Sympathy for barren women narrowed even further in the late nineteenth and early twentieth centuries. That is when medical science decided that the real problem was not the infertile woman's bodily humors or even a malformed cervix—it was her brain. In other words, those who failed to conceive were not just frigid, as the ancients had supposed, but spending too much time thinking. Educating females, said Edwin Clark, author of a new authoritative text, *Sex in Education,* was a recipe for reproductive trouble. "The system does not do two things well at the same time," said Clark, citing the case of Miss A, a dedicated scholar who stood for hours at a time reciting her lessons in class. The accumulated strain, said Clark, "relaxed the sluices of the system," resulting in heavy, painful menstrual periods that left her weak, pale, and twitching—and at risk for permanent sterility. College and career women were literally educating themselves into childlessness.[9]

The body-shaming only grew more intense in the twentieth century. In the opinion of C. G. Child, the physician author of the 1931 text *Sterility and Conception*, barren women were a particularly unlovely set of people—overly brainy academics, psychologically "detached" socialites, or, worse, they were just too fat. Chicago gynecologist William Saul Kroger made the pages of *Time* magazine in 1952 with an article explaining infertility as a woman's "unconscious revulsion" against having a child or, even worse, solid evidence of her "emotional immaturity." Dr. Kroger was also alert to the fact that some of his patients were overweight, more confirmation that somewhere deep down, the true cause of infertility was a "childlike desire to be taken care of."[10] The inability to conceive was in fact nature's first line of defense against unfit mothers.

Old prejudices die hard. The twentieth century saw an explosion of knowledge about hormones, a raft of studies about testosterone, estrogen, and the ovulation cycle. By the 1920s, physicians were already diagnosing tubal blockages and thyroid disorders, and, to the relief of women everywhere, abandoning the invasive surgical techniques popular in the late nineteenth century. Yet, for the average couple, diagnosing and treating infertility was more vexed and time-consuming than ever, as the problem was characterized as a multifaceted condition with a variety of contributing causes, requiring the expertise of endocrinologists, surgeons, and fertility specialists.

Now, in an even more complicated way, infertility is still presented as a choice, and, in fact, a conscious one. New technologies offer never-ending hope—that is, for the privileged few with the requisite amounts of time, money, and emotional durability to press on. There is always another procedure, another test, another biological frontier to be crossed, the once unthinkable becoming safely normal. Test-tube babies are no longer a media sensation; in vitro fertilization is a common procedure covered by most insurance policies. Surrogate mothers and donor insemination do not elicit gasps of moral outrage; they are, after all, the means by which many people, including many same-sex couples, become parents.

The hard truth is that, despite all the advances in medical treatment and social attitudes, no one is guaranteed a child. Today about half the couples who seek treatment will never conceive—an outcome only somewhat better than the two-thirds who never darken the door of a fertility clinic. A stubborn number of cases, like mine, will never end with a baby, much less a definitive "why."

A SINLESS DAY

Now that I am the mother of two wonderful adopted children and the grandmother of three of the most beautiful and winsome little beings the world has ever known, you'd think that none of this would matter. You go through the difficulty, you get the reward.

But it does matter. Once again, I am listening to other people's stories of pregnancy, birth, and lactation, now from the women in my age cohort talking about their daughters and daughters-in-law. I smile gamely through stories of babies coming home and meeting biological siblings, endless speculation about family resemblances and inherited traits. It's still not easy. Even after all those years, I am reliving an old loss, saying another final goodbye to any children I might have conceived, carried, and breastfed.

I feel the same old salt in a still-open wound, though it's different this time around. I no longer believe in instant anything—baby clocks, infertility cures, or personal perfection. I understand that life is not a series of projects to be planned and executed. Complications, even disappointments, are normal. Nor is life a succession of clean breaks, a straight line of progress from one stage to the next. It is what we accumulate, the attitudes and anxieties and strengths that persist over long, long stretches of time.

I have a vivid memory of sitting alone in the backyard of my childhood home on a Sunday afternoon, when I was probably nine or ten years old, and congratulating myself that I had not committed a sin for the entire day. What a triumph! I had made a lie of every Sunday school admonition I had ever heard, the Dutch Calvinist theology that kept me, even as a child, worrying about the eternal consequences of my behavior.

Of course, I realized the fatal error almost instantly. I had committed the sin of pride.

Looking back, I am charmed by the scale of my moral ambitions but also thankful to be free from them. Clearly, life cannot be managed by personal virtue. The ground rules are simply impossible: Perfection is not only unachievable, it is beside the point.

In other words, I now see how those years of childlessness prepared me, in ways both subtle and achingly clear, to be an adult—even a parent. I had to become wiser, stronger, and kinder to myself and to my husband, stop thinking of us as losers or also-rans. We were simply different.

That's not to say that renegotiating your life goals is easy. I was also coming up against my limitations in graduate school, realizing that I would never be a world-class scholar—and, more importantly, that I did not want to be one. I would graduate with my PhD, but all the years of waiting for a baby had pretty much derailed any meaningful foray into the tenure-track job market. When I finally did become a mother, the last thing I wanted to do was send Nate to day care. I had a lot of catching up to do. For many years, I contented myself with part-time junkets, staying afloat in the world of adjunct teaching, reasonably content with its ersatz combination of rewards and indignities. By the time a tenure-track job came around, I took it, only to discover that it did not suit me. I missed the old jury-rigging, my life on the outskirts of academic respectability. In a weird way, I still wanted to wake up every morning and worry on my own about what I needed and what I wanted to do.

I do not expect, or really want, a completely sinless day. My imperfections and failings are old friends, not the kind we invite to parties or write letters to, but the ones who are just always there, instantly recognizable, to me and to the people who know me. I have carved out a space between resignation and resentment, neither dwelling on the past nor closing myself off to it. Perhaps I have learned to give and to accept, now and then, a bit of grace.

Certainly bitterness is a temptation. Schadenfreude is the default emotion of the twenty-first century—just ask a Boston sports fan who loves a Yankee face-plant almost more than a Red Sox victory. Without a doubt, infertility provides plenty of fuel for simmering anger. How could it not? Women have endured centuries of medical theorizing that blamed the sufferer rather than the ailment. But resentment is, in the end, a lazy emotion, an energy sap that leads nowhere. The better possibility, I suggest, is a thoughtful, well-managed state of envy.

That's a complicated idea, I know. Of all the seven deadly sins, it is said, envy brings no pleasure. A sixteenth-century German woodcut depicts this particular sin as a figure literally eating its own heart, devouring it like a delicious piece of fruit. Short of returning to the Garden of Eden, that's about as close to the original human transgression as you can get.

But envy is also a form of desire, albeit a particularly painful one. There is, after all, an element of sadness in it, a "special sort of sorrow," says Thomas Aquinas, "over another's goods."[11] It runs deeper than jealousy, that childish urge to take the lollipop away from the next kid. Envy is a sweet tooth's absolute yearning for satisfaction in a world that offers only kale and broccoli. It keeps us wanting and, in doing so, holds off despair. One of the hardest tricks of being an adult, I've found, is managing my discontent, finding that place beyond cynicism and disappointment, where desire stays alive and, with it, the possibility of transformation.

Somewhere beyond the "toxic positivity" of our self-help culture, our need to find a growth opportunity behind every misfortune, is what Holocaust survivor Victor Frankl called "tragic optimism." We cannot, and should not, deny pain or always try to wriggle free from difficult circumstances, nor do we have to turn every negative emotion into a prayer of gratitude. Traumatic events do not automatically lead to self-improvement. It's what we do with the experience, the difference between a transitory feeling of gratitude—what cancer survivor Kristi Nelson describes as a "momentary emotion"—and a state of gratefulness, an orientation to life that acknowledges the fact of suffering and takes nothing for granted.[12]

The real problem with infertility is the wanting. Without a doubt, it wreaks havoc with a couple's sex life. Is there a worse turnoff than thinking about your eggs when you are supposed to be enjoying yourself? Yet the experience of deprivation, of sitting on the sidelines watching everyone else charging through the goalposts, can also prod you toward what you really want. And that's true for all of us—everyone ends up thwarted by life at least once or twice. The Christian philosopher Thomas Merton describes the feeling of dread, the profound awareness that the worst is likely coming to pass, as an exercise in truthfulness. It lays bare all the ways we are "living a lie," as he says, how we are creating a reality that is manageable, acceptable, and fundamentally false. Truth begins when we drop the entitlement, understand what we truly want, and decide to embrace it.[13] As my other favorite theologian, punk musician Nick Cave, describes the journey of grief after loss, it's "an audacity in the face of things, a kind of reckless refusal to submit to the condition of the world."[14] Maybe the better word is insubordination, a refusal to acquiesce.

What better preparation, then, for meeting your beloved child? That little being, bluntly honest and unimpressed with any of your wonderful achievements, will demand humility from you, one way or another. Any child, adopted or otherwise, will never allow you to live the rest of your life on your own terms. Which is not all bad. In fact, best to begin, I say, with a good head start.

CHAPTER 2

CHILDREN

The first time I saw him, he was peering over the shoulder of a social worker, chewing nonchalantly on a rubber squeeze toy. To this day, the memory is endearing: two dark brown eyes, a tuft of black hair, and a tiny fist wrapped around a bright yellow clam. From the notes and photographs collected by his foster mother, I knew that this little boy had been loved, even cherished, by a close-knit, happy family. And now little Nate was being placed into the hands of complete—and questionably competent—strangers.

It began with a phone call from a cheery social worker. "We have a baby for you," she announced and then proceeded immediately into the particulars. My hands were shaking as I jotted scattered notes about this unknown and soon-to-be beloved little one, five months old, with a Vietnamese birth mother and a white birth father. I dutifully recorded his favorite brand of formula and made a special note that he was also eating applesauce. Still, there was so much I simply didn't know. When I went to buy a jar in the grocery store, it never occurred to me that I should be looking in the baby-food section.

I could not imagine I was worthy. No one is ever ready to become a parent for life, but it helps when you have a due date and nine months to prepare. Yes, we had been thoroughly vetted by the adoption agency. We had sat through seminars and interviews and attested over and over that we were upstanding, responsible adults. I had even quit both of my part-time jobs, just in case the time was near, and started buying baby paraphernalia, albeit cautiously: a pair of tiny little socks, a cute toy or two, stuffed into a bottom drawer for safekeeping. We even took a trip to Europe, a declaration of sorts that this would be the last time for a while that we'd have the money and time to travel.

But most of the time it felt false, a made-up children's story. We were at least theoretically pregnant but, to the naked eye, as childless as ever. In fact, when the telephone rang, I was sitting at home feeling rather foolish, facing a long, empty summer ahead.

Behind it all was an unsayable truth: I wanted a child. I simply yearned for connection with a small one. Yes, the experience of pregnancy and giving birth were never far from my mind, but as the years passed, they had become secondary. These were biological events above and beyond a more fundamental desire. I longed for a child to hold, to talk to and play with, to read bedtime stories to and settle down to sleep—to love.

Why is that still so difficult to say? Some of the problem is mine alone, an aversion to sounding weak and needy, or worse, openly desperate. My particular religious upbringing had conditioned me not to want too much. Our God was not one to be bothered with petty human problems—He was busy enough managing the big stuff, punishing the bad and rewarding the good. Moreover, at some level, I also believed that the adoption agency required a more altruistic motive, something more mindful of the larger social good.

Or maybe it was just the jarring phrase itself. "I want a child," sounds dangerously transactional, as if that little being was yet one more item to bring pleasure and fulfillment, no matter the cost to another person. Just think of the images in popular culture, the deeply unsympathetic infertile women in Margaret Atwood's *The Handmaid's Tale* or P. D. James's *Children of Men*. We are "coached by stories," writes Janice Schroeder, to imagine adoption as a competitive struggle between the "haves and have nots, with the adoptive child as the ultimate 'reward' for parents who cannot conceive on 'their own.'"[1]

I understand now, however, other, deeper reasons for my reticence, a long social conditioning that has contributed much to our contemporary wariness about adoption. It is the way we think about children. Adults can have a hard time remembering that they are beings in their own right, with their own unique will and agency. All too often, we make them a shorthand for our own worries and dreams, as problems to be handled or as projects to be managed, possessions even, to be trained and polished and steered toward success. And behind it all is bottomless fear, to the point of paranoid conspiracy theories about kidnappings, molestation, and murder. Q-Anon's "Pizzagate" narrative is, after all, not just a weird political phenomenon with a frightening grain of truth—it is a deeply disordered fantasy story that adults tell each other about children.

THE CAPABLE CHILD

An obscure but fascinating story from the seventeenth century shows us how far we've traveled, how many of our beliefs about children and childhood mirror twenty-first century hopes and fears, not a universal human experience. Many children of the past, we find, were surprisingly adventurous, self-reliant, and capable.

Thomas Savage was only thirteen years old when he arrived at the Jamestown colony, that infamously doomed outpost in the Virginia wilderness. We know very little about his early life, except that he was very much on his own, a fate not uncommon in seventeenth-century England. Somehow young Thomas had made his way to London and signed on to the Virginia Company's first supply fleet, planning to join the struggling colony as a laborer.[2]

The prospect was no doubt terrifying and exhilarating, the Elizabethan era equivalent of a trip to outer space. We can only imagine the thoughts running through Thomas's mind when, as the ship was being loaded, a bright light appeared in the night sky, the famous Halley's Comet, clearly a portent of unusual and important events to come. The first leg of the trip, which included a stop in the Caribbean, more than lived up to that promise. To a young Englishman raised in fog and drizzle, the New World's brilliant sunshine and its exotic plants and animals would have been a wonder. Virginia proved equally awe-inspiring, an impossibly green land of riverbanks lush with cypress trees, rich black soil, and crabs so large that, it was said, just one could feed four men.

Soon after his arrival in Jamestown, Thomas Savage's life took an even more dramatic turn. He was appointed to a delegation traveling out of the settlement to meet with the Native American sachem Powhatan. The mission was a tricky one: Powhatan was the colonists' most feared enemy, but also a critical source of food and supplies. Anxious to impress but wary of alienating a potential ally, the Englishmen entered Powhatan's village with trumpets blaring, guns and body armor shining in the sun—and a secret diplomatic plan.

In a moment, Thomas Savage's world upended. A hand was on his shoulder, singling him out and pushing him forward. He might have been aware that a transaction was taking place, mostly in signs and signals, but its impact was soon utterly clear. He was being given to this half-clothed frowning stranger as a gift. The reason was intensely practical: Savage was to be a cultural diplomat, a bridge between two alien and potentially hostile worlds.

No doubt, as he watched his comrades depart, leaving him alone among dark-skinned strangers, the boy felt betrayed, bereft, and terrified. Yet, by all accounts, he was treated well, and, over time, he proved himself an asset to both sides, acting as translator and cultural go-between. (Pocahontas, the ten-year-old daughter of Powhatan—who was neither as nubile nor as smitten with John Smith as the Disney legends would have it—played a similar role in reverse.) Savage was certainly physically better off with Powhatan's people than he would have been in Jamestown, a failed experiment already spiraling into tragedy. Beyond that, Thomas may have recognized that life in Powhatan's village was not only easier than he had expected but even a bit familiar. A seventeenth-century English boy would not have been surprised to see all ages and both sexes sleeping in the same room or sharing meals from a single cooking pot. His biggest adjustment would have been hygienic, trading all those layers of English clothing for a simple breechclout and beginning each day with a cold bath in a nearby river.

What's most telling about this story is how improbable it all seems today. A young teenager is about the last person that modern people would trust with intricate cross-cultural détente. They are to us quintessential creatures of the moment, captive to epic mood swings and surging hormonal impulses—not given to complicated adult-style diplomacy. But seventeenth-century people would not have seen Thomas Savage as a feckless teenager. The word itself did not even exist in his day. You started out a child and then became an adult; there was no angst-ridden awkward stage in between.

In fact, Elizabethans believed that young men and women were uniquely pliable, more adaptable than adults to new circumstances—Shakespeare described them as "unbaked and doughy."[3] In that calculation, adventurous, open-minded youths like Savage were particularly suited to New World diplomacy, presumably more able to learn Native languages and absorb Native customs and beliefs and then explain them to the English adults in charge.

Not all that long ago the average child was quite capable. Just like adults, they contributed to the bottom line of the household budget, tending gardens and watching babies, sometimes going out to work for neighbors in shops and factories. Let's be clear, of course—we are not sentimentalizing child labor. The work was tiring and dull and far too often exploitative, poorly paid, and often dangerous. Nor should we think for a moment that no one cared, that the parents of long ago did not love their children as much as we do today. It's tempting to assume that with the high rates of child mortality, people in the past begat one after the other as little expendables, an extra hand in the kitchen or the workroom. There's no need to jump that far. We know from all kinds of accounts that mothers and fathers worried and fussed over their young ones; just like twenty-first-century people, they cherished and nurtured them.

But they also needed their help. Before the advent of unemployment benefits or life insurance, a father's death or incapacity could mean economic catastrophe for an entire family. Before the advent of antibiotics and vaccinations, when every childbirth carried the risk of death and a smallpox epidemic could take out half a town in a matter of weeks, families could not depend on a single breadwinner. And so children worked—on farms, in factories and textile mills, and also in low-paid and dangerous jobs—because they had to. Their mothers and fathers, sisters and brothers, and the wider community depended on them.

In this world, children were miniature adults. Colonial-era parents did not track developmental stages and search for age-appropriate toys and games; their homes had no "naughty corners" or "time-out chairs." Discipline could be harsh—children were, after all, fallen and sinful just like the rest of humanity and required a strong adult hand to teach them obedience and respect. But they were community members nonetheless.

Here's another historical reality: Until fairly recently, the vast majority of children did not grow to adulthood under the parental roof. In fact, none but the very privileged expected to spend every day from infancy onward carefully nurtured by their biological mother and father. Moving from one household to another, working for neighbors or relatives, was normal and expected or, as the authors of a historical survey put it, "neither unusual nor remarkable."[4] In the colonial era, boys left home to learn a trade, living in the care of a master who was bound to teach them a useful skill and also ensure that they could read, write, and "cipher." Girls practiced the intricacies of colonial housewifery with their mothers or by working alongside a mistress who was often a family member or a neighbor.

The colonial work ethic spared no one, except the very rich. Even some of the wealthier sort paid a fee to apprentice their sons to lawyers or doctors or silversmiths. The more middling types entered into contracts to have their children sent to other farm households, sometimes because they could not trust themselves to be adequately strict. Pauper or "bastard" children, some as young as three or four, were routinely—and legally—put to work, bound out to labor for a master who agreed to house and feed them.

The system worked, more or less, because of who was watching. Today, such unsentimental arrangements look like an invitation to abuse, leaving vulnerable orphans in the care of adults with little incentive for coddling them. And certainly, as anyone who has read a Charles Dickens novel knows, life could be both brutish and short for the poor and parentless. Yet there were crucial safeguards. The colonial system was based on the so-called poor laws of Elizabethan England, which required local communities to take on the burden of care for the destitute. Even pauper children were legally protected by contracts, and, perhaps even more crucially, their masters were under the scrupulous oversight of local authorities—the overseers of the poor and the town magistrate.

People recognized the communal benefit. Back then, both children and adults depended on others to help with the perennially difficult task of turning fractious children into responsible adults, then as now a dark and dangerous passage. What we might see as an ingenious device for farming out a noxious adolescent was actually preparing a child for successful adulthood. In fact, rehoming one's children was the responsible thing to do: Only an outsider, it was thought, could provide the strict, unsentimental discipline necessary for future success.

And let's remember that parents were not leaving their children in the hands of strangers. In a premodern world, before factories and railroads and sprawling cities, people tended to know each other fairly well. Daily life in a colonial-era village, writes historian John Demos, brought a "density of human contact that is hard even to imagine today," a "tight web of social experience" that was lived out in public spaces—churches, marketplaces, and courtrooms. Though "pre-modern communities had their share of nonconformists, eccentrics, and criminals," says Demos, there were "no isolates, no habitual strangers."[5]

Respect for childhood independence only deepened as the American colonies became a nation, boasting a democratic constitution and a corresponding set of beliefs and values. In the Old World, the young were subordinate to the old, hemmed in by rules and tradition. In the New World, each child was a "little citizen," a person with the capacity for independent thought and action. "Probably nowhere in the Western world," writes historian Paula Fass, "could one visit the homes of respectable families and find children who so easily took part in the family circle and were so comfortably regarded as equals, not as subordinates or dependents."[6] Enlisting children's help made sense in a new nation with lots of work to do and a chronic labor shortage. But in the early years of the nineteenth century, as the national character began to solidify, the capable, hardworking child was also a living testimony to the promise of American democracy.

At this point, though, we need to stop and realize how differently childhood played out for those in bondage in the American South. The deepest offense to the children born and raised under slavery was not that they went out and worked in the fields—that was the rule on every farm, in both North and South. It was the indignity of forced labor that promised nothing, that punished the very qualities of self-respect and initiative that offered European American parents and children pride and satisfaction.

One particularly poignant story comes from "Elizabeth," who was raised on a plantation at the turn of the nineteenth century. She was nearly a hundred years old when she told her story in 1863, but her childhood memories were sharp, fresh, and painful. Elizabeth was barely eleven years old when her master sent her off to work at a distant farm, and she suffered intensely. "I grew so lonely and sad," she said, "I thought I should die, if I did not see my mother." When the overseer refused to let her go back for a visit, Elizabeth left on her own, walking the twenty miles by herself. But the reunion was brief. Her mother only let her stay a short while before she sent the girl back to her new master. Their words at parting were sharp and painful: Elizabeth now had "nobody in the wide world to look to but God." And there was plenty of trouble ahead. "On reaching the farm," Elizabeth recalled, "I found the overseer was displeased at me for going without his liberty. He tied me with a rope, and gave me some stripes of which I carried the marks for weeks."[7]

Enslaved children were material property, one movable piece in larger economic transactions. In the 1850s alone, of the roughly 270,000 slaves sold to cotton plantations in the Deep South, nearly half were children and teenagers. Parents had no formal control over even the most basic matters, much less the sanctioning power of a surrounding moral community. Owners decided whether mothers and fathers could cohabit and where their children would stay—and whether they would grow old together. "Knowing that a child's chance of being sold increased as he or she grew older," writes historian Wilma King, affected even the smallest act. "Like stepping on a land mine in a war zone, any faux pas committed by the children could have disastrous results."[8]

Elizabeth's story, and those of untold thousands of children under slavery, are more than simply outrageous and sad. The neglect and callousness she endured, and the appalling contrast to the freedom given other children, demonstrate our willingness to tolerate deep contradictions in our attitudes about childhood.

Who is responsible for our children? Does the obligation belong to parents or to society—or to no one? The questions we struggle with today go back nearly two centuries. As nineteenth-century American society grew more complex, more urban, and more scattered, those questions grew more painful and complex. The old safety net, the close-knit communities that kept tabs on the poor and orphaned, frayed and weakened. It was one thing to put children out to work when small communities knew who was where and what was what, and something entirely different in a big and complicated city. If families failed and neighbors proved indifferent, who would see that the very young were fed and clothed and kept safe from exploitation?

THE STRANGER'S CHILD

For a while, orphanages were the best answer. Today the word conjures up all kinds of problematic images—we think of wan children scrubbing floors, rows of tiny beds in windowless rooms, prim matrons and cruel overseers happily withholding a second helping of watery gruel from a hungry child. Yet two hundred years ago, they were a novel humanitarian experiment, an ambitious combination of home, school, and financial aid for families in crisis.[9]

The first American orphanages were founded in the early nineteenth century, almost all of them by women acting out of deeply idealistic motives. They were determined to nest every poor or orphaned child in a home or as close an approximation as they could manage. In those early days, the ideal orphanage was a collection of small cottages, each with a live-in matron. The residents worked, as did most children, but not for pay or for outsiders. In fact, one of the founders' major purposes was to protect the parentless from the old *binding out* system, which simply put them to work on a farm or in a shop without much care or training. The goal was for each child to become a self-supporting adult, equipped with a strong work ethic and a good set of practical skills. It's also worth noting that orphanages were often temporary solutions: A good proportion of the children were "half orphans," surrendered by a parent unable to support them but hoping for better times ahead. Many went back to their parents or a near relative.[10]

From the start, there were challenges. The well-intentioned women managing early nineteenth-century orphanages confronted a sea of unknowns and ambiguities, especially when it came to trusting the good intentions of a stranger. They could not be sure that the mothers and children they so urgently pitied were actually telling the truth. Take, for example, the story of little Hannah Flovell, whose aunt piously insisted to the managers of the Boston Female Asylum that the child had been abandoned by her widowed mother and "exposed to the vilest precepts and examples Imagination could paint." Fairly quickly, however, the story fell apart. It appeared that Hannah's mother was paying the aunt for childcare while she went off to look for work; when the money stopped coming, the little girl was summarily packed off to the orphanage. The managers understood the bait and switch, but they agreed anyway and even took Hannah in again later when her mother, still penniless and out of work, returned with the child and requested her readmission.[11]

Deciding who merited help and who did not was never easy, and, as city populations expanded, the task became impossible. Growing up is never easy, but imagine, for a moment, what it was like in a place like Chicago: In 1860, it was the nation's eighth largest city, with a population of just over a hundred thousand; fifty years later, in 1910, the population had reached two million, even after a devastating fire in 1871. Poverty and deadly epidemics were only part of the challenge of surviving to adulthood in a nineteenth-century city. Simply knowing your neighbors was getting complicated. Many—most—of the urban newcomers were immigrants from Europe, with different languages and different customs.

There were just too many people, too many stories of desperation to validate, tens of thousands of children living on the streets in New York City alone.[12] The Civil War brought even more family dislocation. According to one estimate, almost half of American children who lived during that era lost at least one parent before they reached twenty.[13]

This meant turning to friends or relatives when you needed a place for a child to go, or sometimes relying on the kindness of random strangers. For a while, especially in small-town America, trust was still possible.

Billy Sunday was twelve years old when his mother sent him and an older brother, Ed, to the Soldiers' Orphanage in Glenwood, Iowa. Mrs. Sunday had been pregnant with Billy, her third child, when her husband went off to join the Twenty-Third Iowa Infantry Volunteers. He died in a Missouri army camp a month after Billy was born.[14]

Many years later, when Billy Sunday was a household name as a world-famous evangelist notorious for his aggressive showmanship—he liked to throw chairs at the devil, as the story goes—he remembered every detail of their hard goodbye. Mrs. Sunday's eyes were red, and her hair was disheveled, Billy recalled, on that sad afternoon when he, his brother, and their mother walked together to the Ames, Iowa, train station, one of her arms around Billy and the other around Ed. The two boys rode alone through the night to Council Bluffs, a trip of about 160 miles on a modern highway. All they had was a letter of introduction to the orphanage superintendent; no money for food and no place to sleep when the train made an overnight stop along the way.

And so Billy and Ed relied on the kindness of strangers. A cook at a nearby hotel found out that they were heading for an orphanage and gave them lunch and dinner. "My husband was a soldier," she said, "and he never came back. He wouldn't turn any one away and I wouldn't turn you boys away." When the train conductor discovered Billy and Ed hiding in the caboose of the freight train heading for Glenwood, he was ready to throw them off until he learned where they were going. He saw the tears running down their faces and started crying along with them. "Just sit still boys," he said. "It won't cost a cent to ride on my train."[15]

Billy and Ed were effectively orphans for two years. When they returned home in 1876, Ed was old enough to support himself, and Billy, more help around the house, less of a burden on his mother and new stepfather. In the meantime, he had also learned to read, write, and do some math. Although Billy would carry the scars of separation for the rest of his life, he was well aware that the education he had received at the orphanage was far better than that he would have managed to get at home. More than that, he had learned to work hard and take care of himself. "I was taught to do my best," he said, adding that "More people fail from lack of purpose than from lack of opportunity."[16]

I think it's safe to say that none of these living conditions for children would meet our approval today. We find it hard to imagine handing over a vulnerable child to an unfamiliar adult, much less letting anyone under twenty to fend completely for themselves. The level of social trust seems impossible.

But at the time, with a problem so huge, with so many children desperate for help, even the people who cared pushed the boundaries in surprising, sometimes downright unnerving ways.

ORPHANS ON TRAINS

Charles Loring Brace, who founded the Children's Aid Society (CAS) in 1853, was a tireless promoter of "child welfare" in an age that was deeply unsentimental about poor people and broken families. He is now, however, roundly vilified for his solution to child poverty. Brace is best known, and infamous, for his "orphan trains," the literal vehicles of what was called the *placing-out* system, the practice of sending thousands of poor children from East Coast cities to farms in the Midwest. By the time the system fell into disrepute in the 1930s, some 150,000 children had left their homes in cities, many never to return.[17]

In the early days at least, few people considered this kidnapping. Many of the children were actually brought in by parents who saw an opportunity for a better future; the rest were orphans or assumed to be budding criminals, referred to Brace by the court system.[18] In fact, the public was generally sympathetic, doing a bit of moral math and deciding the orphan trains were best for all concerned. What sickly, deprived city child wouldn't prefer a life in the fresh open air of the Midwestern countryside? And for that matter, why would the comfortable argue with vaguely statistical evidence of success? No one was scandalized that young children—poor ones anyway—were being sent off to the labor force. Except for the very well off, working for a living was still commonplace, the expected fate for the less fortunate.[19]

Still, the details are genuinely unsettling. Brace essentially did away with the old system of apprenticeship contracts and community oversight. Moreover, though the children usually traveled in groups under the care of CAS staff, and though they had to accept a placement willingly, the experience had to have been harrowing. The trains would stop in a town and the orphans taken to a church or a courthouse, where they were lined up for viewing and selection by the local farmers. Some went home with a family while others boarded the train once again and traveled on to the next town. Certainly there was ample risk of exploitation and abuse, not to mention searing emotional pain when brothers and sisters were separated. Though the recordkeeping is not entirely trustworthy, we can be sure that many children never saw their biological families again.

Late nineteenth-century American society did not believe that every parent could—or should—be allowed to raise their own children. But the alternative, letting the authorities take charge, opened the door to cruelties that we still struggle to grasp.

The government officials and Christian missionaries who organized and staffed schools for Native American children believed they were helping to civilize and save tribes in the path of white settlement. Richard Pratt, founder of the Carlisle School in Pennsylvania in 1879, openly declared his goal, to "kill the Indian" and "save the man." In many ways, the Native American schools were like orphanages—children acquired a rudimentary education and vocational skills meant to turn them into economically self-sufficient adults. But they were also submitted to deep indignities, forced to cut their hair and adopt white dress and customs, and prohibited from speaking their Native languages. This callousness, we now know, could also be lethal. Recently, the discovery of hundreds of unmarked graves in Canada, containing the remains of First Nations children sent to government boarding schools, has led to accusations of "cultural genocide" by its Truth and Reconciliation Commission. The historian Preston McBride has documented at least a thousand deaths at just four schools in the United States, between 1879 and 1934, most from disease or neglect. He estimates that the actual number is far higher, perhaps forty thousand children, a mass-casualty event on the order of the infamous Trail of Tears.[20]

No one defends Charles Loring Brace now, much less Indian schools or even orphanages—and perhaps that's the point. Those attempts were already pushing the boundaries of social trust about as far as they could go in the nineteenth century, too far in fact. For plenty of good reasons, we no longer approve of parceling out children to strangers.

Turn-of-the-century American society had an enormous challenge to face: While social reformers campaigned for moral reform and the prohibition of alcohol, the fact was that the greatest damage to children came from poverty and inequality—a cold truth that almost no one wanted to face. Then, as now, it was easier to blame vice and criminality on the bad behavior of the poor than to tackle the deeper problems of economic injustice. By the late 1800s, the care of needy children had become a haphazard system, a hodgepodge of informal, unsupervised, and unregulated arrangements. The lucky ones ended up taken in by neighbors or relatives. Others were prey to an underground network of "baby farms" that warehoused young children for profit. There, the mortality rates were chilling. In Chicago, in the early twentieth century, only half of infants born survived; in Baltimore, it was less than one-third. But what to do? The task of regulating this sprawling hodgepodge was left to nonprofit organizations, such as the Society for the Prevention of Cruelty to Children or to struggling and underfunded state boards of charity. In the meantime, the horror stories proliferated. Opportunities for abuse and exploitation went largely unchecked.[21]

The early twentieth century, the so-called Progressive Era, was a time of great optimism about big solutions for social problems. In 1912 the government established the US Children's Bureau within the Department of Labor and in 1921 passed the Sheppard–Towner Act, which, until it was repealed in 1928, provided public health nurses to women in rural areas. Another possibility was providing subsidies to poor mothers, to keep families together and children out of orphanages. The plan made sense and directly benefited the most needy; by 1920 some forty states had established "mothers' pensions." But committing to this much direct financial support was a big hurdle for the American public, who generally recoiled from the suggestion that maternal love had a monetary value. How could you offer a woman payment for carrying out her most sacred obligation?

The economic emergency of the 1930s gave rise to another set of government programs aimed at keeping families intact: the Social Security Act, specifically Title IV, known as Aid to Dependent Children (ADC), later AFDC. These initiatives would change many lives for the better, certainly, allowing many families to stay together despite economic hardship. But these programs were not meant to provide a long-term solution to the more fundamental problem, the spiraling consequences of poverty and the resulting breakdown of the family.

Government subsidies came with the clear understanding that they were temporary—and they were not available for everyone. Racial animus on top of longstanding cultural anxieties about paying for maternal care dramatically limited the support available to Black parents and children.

Bureaucratic hurdles abounded. In Cook County, Illinois, the heart of Black Chicago, an unmarried mother received aid only if she could prove she was already maintaining a "suitable" home, had genuine financial need, and was ready and willing to take legal action against her child's father. In other words, she had to show the government that she was actually capable of supporting herself without outside help. During the post–World War II era, a time when the number of illegitimate births was soaring across the US, Black women received a declining share of ADC benefits. The stereotyping had begun, that they were undeserving, insufficiently grateful, and unworthy of public support.[22]

The foster care system is another part of this legacy of tepid and temporary government support for people in need. Title V of the Social Security Act was designed to keep the poor and orphaned out of institutions, providing money to allow them to board with families. The program remained fairly stable and contributed to the almost complete disappearance of orphanages by the 1940s and 1950s. But in the 1960s and 1970s exploding numbers of needy children as well as struggling families, followed by the drug epidemics of the 1980s and 1990s burdened the system to its limits.[23]

There are so many ways to talk about foster care and its problems—the literature is vast, as they say in academia. But the all-too-brief summary I've provided already tells us plenty about the consequences. The children and teenagers in foster care today are wedged between old contradictions. The government has a vested interest in keeping families together whenever possible, a legacy that goes back to the Progressive Era. At the same time, because the government has been run overwhelmingly by wealthy white men, it contains a deep distrust of non-white and non-wealthy parents. Over time it has become easier for those in power to look away and allow the vulnerable to become invisible. And so we find that nearly one-third of the nation's unhoused population grew up in foster care, as did a fifth of the prison population under age thirty. Only 6 percent of foster children will have completed either a two- or four-year college degree by the time they are forty.[24]

You would think that adoption would be especially appropriate for foster children, that it would even be key to their future success. For a long time, however, it was technically difficult for foster parents to adopt a foster child, even if the child was a blood relative. Before a foster parent could adopt, they had to first win custody from the birth parent and then be willing to relinquish the financial support they had been receiving. For people with limited resources and for children with special needs, those hurdles were especially high. Since the late 1990s the system has undergone reform, especially regarding the possibility of adoption. The Promoting Safe and Stable Families legislation of 2001 was an attempt to speed adoptions and remove race as a factor in placements. But because adoption is primarily subject to state rather than federal law, the changes have been piecemeal.

Foster care, however, is one of the problems facing children and families today. The vast inequalities of wealth and our fraying social safety net have visited some of their worst effects on the very young; our children live with the consequences. Today one child out of seven lives below the poverty line, nearly three-quarters of them Black or brown. American children today are the most vulnerable to homelessness: one-third live in households where more than 30 percent of the family income goes toward rent or a mortgage. And as every parent likely knows, childcare can be prohibitively expensive: In 2019, across more than half the country, infant care was more costly than public college tuition.[25] In so many places in the United States it is very, very hard to be a child.

EMOTIONAL TOKENS

It's also important to place the long history of child poverty in America—the orphan trains and baby farms, the horrors faced by children under slavery and in government schools—alongside another very different set of changes. These stories of deprivation and abuse are particularly devastating when we remember how life was changing for the better for so many others in the nineteenth century, particularly the rising middle classes. The Victorian era gave us "home, sweet home," burdening posterity with all kinds of unrealistic expectations about familial harmony and parental bliss. Home was the place where fathers returned after a long day slogging through the masculine world of business, industry, and competitive capitalism. It was to be a sacred space for moral rearming and emotional repair, a peaceful retreat where women and children lived quietly apart. They were, theoretically at least, not deemed to be "working"—that is, not contributing to the household's bottom line.

In this arrangement, children were no longer capable people with a particular set of responsibilities but beautiful, fragile beings, "emotional tokens," as one historian puts it, who required unstinting love by devoted parents.[26] Unlike the offspring of their puritan predecessors who were rebellious beings born in sin, Victorian children were innocents who required not harsh punishment or warnings of hell, but consistent and sensitive nurture by godly mothers and fathers.

In fact, by the turn of the century, many Americans were coming around to the idea that preteen children had a right *not* to work. As Felix Adler, the warm-hearted liberal founder of the Society for the Study of Child Nature, wrote in 1905, profiting from the labor of a child was "to touch profanely a sacred thing."[27]

Today, in the average American home, child labor is mostly symbolic, a set of chores meant to teach responsibility and rewarded with token pay. Three-year-old Tommy helps unload the dishwasher, handing dishes to the parent, who stows them in their proper places. Little Suzie laboriously matches the socks in the laundry basket, a task her mother or father could finish in minutes. Their work is not valuable—and that's the point, really. Our children are, as historian Viviana Zelizer has described them, "priceless." They have no economic value—if anything, a child is a burden on the family budget—but their emotional worth is beyond calculation. We love them without limits, without boundaries.[28]

Without a doubt, this cultural shift was an important benefit to many. By the early twentieth century, it was becoming a little easier, on the whole, to be a child. Stricter labor laws meant more years of schooling and greater opportunities for humane, comfortable lives. Even the hierarchical rules of family relationships were moderating, as the old Victorian ideal—the authoritarian paterfamilias and submissive, sentimental mother—gave way to a warmer, more informal and emotionally intelligent one. In the twentieth century, corsets and fancy parlors would be replaced by T-shirts and family rooms and Dr. Spock. Children were valued not as miniature adults or as innocent, angelic beings, but as a special kind of human being with a unique view of the world.

Yet, from what I hear and see, being a parent is more fraught than ever. When I take my grandchildren to the neighborhood playground in my semiurban Boston neighborhood, the parent talk is about achievements, a toddler's precocious vocabulary or her miraculous agility on the monkey bars. Grandmothers do not care for such things, of course. My own somewhat feral suburban upbringing allowed all kinds of freedom. We left the house on bicycles in the morning and came home when my mother rang the dinner bell. But grandmothers also know that even the most promising offspring will take their parents down a notch or two before they are finished with them. Ultimately, every child is an enigma wrapped in a mystery, and the less a parent can predict, the better for all concerned.

Perhaps I should be more sympathetic. We are nervous about our children now and, in many cases, rightly so. We live in complicated, unsentimental times, with a modern set of dangers our ancestors could not have begun to imagine—Instagram and fentanyl, school shootings and suicide. Trust feels in short supply. Most of us have no idea what our neighbors are doing behind their four walls, and the ubiquitous news cycle suggests a lot of dangerous possibilities. Online stalkers, child pornographers, and gunmen with AR-15s threaten havoc on all of us.

Yet we live in one of the safest societies for children ever devised, having mostly eradicated childhood diseases and put in place national standards for safe food and water. Not all that long ago, it was perfectly fine to spice up the taste of milk with formaldehyde; no one gave a second thought about car seats, even seat belts. Still, no one feels safe. As writer Judith Warner points out, more than half the parents in a 1997 survey worried that their children would be victims of violent crime; a few years later, in 2000, the number had risen to three-fourths—despite a well-publicized drop in national crime rates. A third of American households believed that at least one member had a food allergy, even though the actual incidence in the population at large is less than 1 percent.[29]

If anything, the fear has grown more grotesque: Presidential candidates are rumored to be murdering children and drinking their blood in the basements of pizza parlors; cabals of kindergarten teachers are secretly "grooming" their students to service the sexually deviant. We cast the gimlet eye upon them all—preschool teachers and Boy Scout leaders, kindly uncles and church youth pastors—and demand a background check.

We have also imposed new benchmarks for success and penalties for failure. While earlier generations worried about scarlet fever or accidents with pitchforks and mowing machines, modern ones face the possibility of not loving their children enough or in the right way and thus inflicting lifelong debilitating personality disorders on their young. Modern mothers and fathers learn their roles from certified professionals, warm yet authoritative figures like Dr. Spock and T. Berry Brazelton. They are to watch their children like hawks, measuring and inspecting and comparing, from the first moment in the delivery room on through young adulthood, tracking a child's progress against national standards, not just for height and weight but for key developmental milestones like crawling, walking, and talking.

The attention has its benefits, of course. Proactive medical and psychological care have afforded countless families and children better, easier, and longer lives. But the demand for control—or the illusion that it is possible—has made modern parenting, "nothing less than perfect madness," as Warner puts it, a futile, painful exercise in micromanagement. Ironically, the anxiety is sharpest in families with the financial and educational means to expect their children to be winners, to finish the rat race with Ivy League degrees and thick investment portfolios. "It is as though, through the power of our prodigious mental energies, we feel we can erect a protective force field around our children," sheltering them against failure. "And if this doesn't work," says Warner, "then the fault lies with us, so we must try harder. Do better. Be *there* more—and more perfectly."[30]

These complicated fears about the welfare of our children are tender places where adoption presses us, laying open all the confused and contradictory ways we think about them. On the one hand is the priceless child, the emotional token, of whom no adult is fully worthy, and on the other, the invisible children who remind us of how much our social ties have frayed, of our lost sense of obligation to the stranger's child. No wonder adoption has become challenging, a fraught and complicated process involving adoption agencies, social workers, lawyers, and, of course, financial costs.

There is no doubt that Americans today love children: Witness all the money and time we spend on amusing, protecting, and educating them. But that's not the whole story. Certainly, fears about pedophiles and faulty playground equipment are warranted, but it's also true that much of the hype and hysteria are just noise, a big staticky distraction that obscures a deeper problem. Americans today, says Paula Fass, need a larger vision, one that "embraces all the nation's children." Parents would do well to develop "a sturdier confidence in their own progeny," in tandem with an understanding that "our children's future depends on the common good of all."[31] We lack something we desperately need: that ancient skill of being able to care for other people's children, to learn to love a stranger's child as our own.

There are plenty of strangers' children who need our attention. Epidemics in our own time, from AIDS to COVID-19 to opioids, not to mention wars and climate catastrophes, have created millions of orphans. Some 10.5 million children worldwide were orphaned as a result of COVID alone. In the United States, by the spring of 2022, the COVID pandemic had left 200,000 children, the vast proportion of them Hispanic, Black, and Native American, without at least one parent. Add to that the horrific impact of opioid addiction: Between 2011 and 2021, more than 320,000 children lost a parent to drug addiction. This is a side of the overdose epidemic that "we really don't speak much about," says Dr. Nora Volkow, director of the National Institute on Drug Abuse.[32]

It's one thing to celebrate your own progeny, something much more to care about children in general. I admit that my own hard-earned experience, my years of not being a parent when I deeply wanted to be one, might have made me more critical of other parents than I ought to be. I wonder sometimes whether any of those anxious playground parents are able to sit back and simply enjoy being around children. By no means do I discount the concerns of careful parents—like most adoptive mothers, I have experienced high levels of angst about my children's emotional welfare.

Yet I still wonder if our children are stronger and more capable than we give them credit for.

ENIGMA

I collect images of mystery. The walls of my study are dotted with reminders that there's more to life than I can see—rivers winding off into nothingness, birch trees contemplating a sunset, and ships moored against endless horizons. My favorites, though, are portraits of people, all of them long dead. One is of a group of elderly Civil War veterans, lined up in full uniform, in the town of Boothbay Harbor, Maine. I look at them and wonder: What horrors lie behind those tight Yankee faces? What might they be remembering or trying to forget?

Another photo shows a group of young mine workers from Calumet Harbor, Michigan, boys barely into their teens posing with their picks and shovels and lunch buckets. Their determined expressions leave me with a mixture of respect and sadness: Nineteenth-century copper mining was not a kind business, even for full-grown men. And as much as I want to believe otherwise, it's very likely that those children were living hard lives and that things didn't get any easier as they became adults.

Photographs of children like this one are double mysteries. There is so much we can never know about the past, but of all the people who have lived before us, children are the most obscure. They are the real strangers in every time and place.

It's one of those inescapable roadblocks between past and present. Any questions we ask about children are fundamentally unanswerable. What thoughts were going through the minds of those children heading off on orphan trains? Were they worried or excited, sad or relieved? All that we can know is secondhand at best, filtered through the gauze of adult memories or recorded by doting, critical, thoughtless, or well-intentioned grown-ups. Children, especially those who are not able to read or write, cannot tell their own stories directly. In the end, we hit the proverbial brick wall: All of the information we have about children and childhood in the past comes from outsiders, from adults.

Historians have learned to take all kinds of other secondhand accounts with a grain of salt; we are wary of men writing about women, whites writing about Black and brown people, the native-born writing about immigrants. We work hard to correct those biased accounts with authentic first-person voices. Yet, in history, as in present-day life, children have demanded our humility.

Somehow, though, grown-ups still believe they always know what is best for children. While it's true that there are plenty of decisions children should never have to make on their own and plenty of capable grown-ups to do so, a child is not, as most parents eventually learn, a one-way street, a passive little object who receives our nurture with quiet gratitude. Every little one is our partner in an ongoing—and culture-creating—give-and-take. Bit by bit, in the complex negotiations that go into everything from a family trip to the grocery store to the orchestration of Christmas morning, children make history.

As an adoptive parent, I have thought a lot about the mysteriousness of children. Early on, I couldn't even begin to predict whether my little ones would be musical geniuses or jocks, writers or mathletes. At first I wanted to scrutinize every act and interaction in an attempt to figure out what that voiceless being had in store. But at some point I realized I could also relax my grip, watch and wait, and accept the mysteries lying dormant in my bundle of joy.

Far from being flawed or invisible, adopted children have something important to teach us. We stereotype them as damaged people, incomplete, perhaps even coping with trauma, but really we owe them a thorough hearing. Betty Jean Lifton, an adoptee, a writer, and a psychologist, speaks of them as "twice-born" people, with two sets of parents, two different stories, two realities. That doubleness, as she describes it, is confusing, painful, and isolating—stressful enough to invite significant problems with mental health.[33] Nicole Chung, a Korean adoptee who grew up in rural Oregon, writes that "a wide sea seemed to separate the lone island of my experience from the well-mapped continents on which other people, other families resided." Even the best-intended cannot, she says, "possibly understand how much my adoption had given me; how much it had taken away."[34]

Living two realities at once is not easy. "I am often told that I am lucky," writes Elizabeth Spiers, a *New York Times* columnist, "that I got a 'second chance' and that I should be grateful my adoptive parents took me in. People who say these things are often well intentioned, but what they are saying is patronizing and wrong. I am not particularly lucky, or I wouldn't have had to be adopted in the first place."[35]

How do you reconcile resentment and gratitude, love and bitterness? How do you negotiate between two sets of obligation, two sets of social expectation? "There is no point in denying that it is different to grow up knowing that your mother is not actually your mother, and that your father is not actually your father, but nonetheless they are your mother and father," writes Scottish poet Jackie Kay. "Those seeming opposites—How can someone be your mother and not your mother? How can somebody be real and not be real?—are at the heart of what it means to be adopted; you have to contain both these supposed opposites together."[36]

THE CHOOSING

Suddenly I understand why my daughter quotes Walt Whitman at the top of her Facebook page: "I contain multitudes." The poet accepts the paradox of what it means to be human, writing, "You say I contradict myself? Very well, I contradict myself."

Anna came just before Christmas. Born in September, she was a one-in-a-million perfect match to our unique family, a little Amerasian girl to join our Amerasian son. Of course, there were wrinkles to be ironed out. We learned in mid-December that the agency wanted to do another search for her birth father, a process that would require at least a couple of months before we could legally adopt her. And so we had a decision to make: We could take Anna home as our foster child and possibly lose her if her birth father turned up, or we could wait until the search was done, in February or March.

The choice was not difficult. With only a few days to prepare, and in the throes of Christmas celebrations, we buckled a second car seat into our Subaru and set off to meet our new daughter and sister. We would take her home that very same day.

The birth father question was not the only wrinkle, however. Baby Anna had a shock of dark hair, a round little face, a button nose—and a severely crossed right eye. In the hurry of the holidays, the agency had not prepared us for this obvious imperfection or for the years of doctor visits and surgery ahead. They did not warn us about the clueless staring and the reams of unsolicited advice we would receive from family, friends, and perfect strangers.

But back on that December day, Anna couldn't have cared less. While I held her and fed her a bottle, my eyes searching for the right contact with hers, a little hand reached up and circled my finger. I felt something change, as if this determined baby had also made a decision. We were hers.

We would be hers as we sorted through the painful swings of childhood, a fierce desire for independence and an equally intense drive for attachment. Life seemed to bounce from suddenly aborted sleepovers with grade school friends to equally sudden trips to Germany, Big Sur, and other parts unknown. And with every joggle and twist, we were more hers than ever. We were hers during her ups and downs, cycles of euphoria and sadness. We still belong—we cannot, do not want to, imagine any other possibility.

CHAPTER 3

KIN

"Wait a minute." Seven-year-old Anna looked intently across the dinner table. "If the Rosenbergs had adopted me, I'd be Jewish, right?"

"Well, yeah," I answered cautiously. The Rosenbergs, our landlords, lived upstairs, and Anna played with their daughter Rachel almost every day. The family was intensely observant as well as welcoming, and so Anna was no stranger to Shabbat services and Purim rituals. Every fall she and Rachel played in the backyard Succoth, and at Passover, we received grocery bags of leavened bread and rolls cleared from the Rosenbergs' kitchen shelves. And now Anna was sitting down to a dinner of store-bought meatballs and spaghetti, blessed by a Protestant grace given by her Protestant minister father.

I don't remember the rest of the conversation, except that I was vague and noncommittal. Knowing Anna, I was pretty sure that the "How did I end up here with you?" question would be asked more than once. I would have plenty more chances to work out a nuanced, thoughtful answer.

In the meantime, we would live with the mystery, that big open question about why we had become a family. Certainly we did not match, racially or religiously. Nathan's birth parents were Buddhist and Catholic; Anna's parents' religions are murkier but probably much the same. So what was the logic behind our being together, if any?

Some people compare adoption to a particular kind of marriage, those charmed pairings that begin with love at first sight. "When I held him/her in my arms for the first time," so the story goes, "there was no question that we belonged together." And everything that happens afterward proves that first big hunch. Our lucky and predestined couple remains deeply in love, without an instant of doubt or a moment of regret.

I am far too pragmatic for such rash behavior. My husband and I courted, got engaged, then unengaged, then engaged again, and in the end we went to the altar believing that we were doing a good thing. In the decades that followed, we learned and unlearned and relearned how to be the kind of people who become good husbands and wives. As with many marriages, our commitment to love each other has proven itself over and over again as the years have gone by, though not without some periodic applications of emotional elbow grease.

The same holds true for adoption. I confess that I am flummoxed by people, some already with biological children, who blandly insist that they would "really like to adopt some day," as if it were as simple as going to Walmart for a jar of peanut butter. That prospect is far more daunting than most of us realize, from that first moment of meeting onward, through all the years ahead, as utter strangers learn to become kin.

Our story of becoming a family is so different, a strange mix of the exciting and the perfunctory. We met our beloved children in the most ordinary setting, the anodyne waiting room of an office complex. We became parents while sitting on a Naugahyde sofa under the cold glare of fluorescent lighting—an emotional experience like no other but hardly comparable to the dramatic, sweaty climax of childbirth.

The ambiguities widened over time. Even today, I want to make sure everyone out there understands that we are just as normal as any other family, just as "real." Sometimes I have had to insist, to family members and teachers, that our children are not maladjusted or weird because they had different biological parents. They don't walk down the street in some special adopted way, and we don't wake up every morning as adoptive parents. We go through life's joys and struggles just like everybody else. But I also want people to respect the fact that my family is not like theirs. I want them to see what they take for granted, to understand the scale of difficulty of our outwardly normal lives, the particular ways we bump up against hurts and tend to losses.

In our family, for example, birthday celebrations carry a particular emotional punch. We have no memories of a pregnancy or delivery room; there's no reminiscing about labor or breastfeeding or coming home from the hospital. Instead, I am sharply aware that, for another woman, the day is likely an occasion for grief. And so we have another quiet celebration on adoption anniversaries, when we can reminisce about Naugahyde couches and office waiting rooms. There have also been times when even that day was too tender, and we allowed it to pass quietly. In other words, we live as if we are a family formed by blood ties, while we know full well that this is a ruse, sometimes even a performance.

This careful negotiation of celebrations and anniversaries is not a game we made up ourselves. The ambiguities we negotiate are the product of centuries, the end result of years of effort to reduce risk and impose order. The project began in the early twentieth century, when well-meaning people worked very hard to convince the skeptics that adoptive families were absolutely no different from biological ones and believed they could engineer them to succeed. That complicated legacy is still with us. Yet in the end, all that hard work of normalizing only made things more complicated, harder for outsiders to understand and for insiders to explain. And so we wonder: Is it kinder to treat adoptive families differently? Or is it best for all concerned to overlook the obvious distinction? Family life is hard enough without an extra layer of confusion.

FAMILIES BY LAW

Adoption, as a legal category, did not exist in the United States until 1851. That's when the Massachusetts General Court passed the Act to Provide for the Adoption of Children, a first attempt to fix a messy and increasingly haphazard informal system of child custody. Before 1851, at least as far as the law was concerned, taking in someone else's child was mostly a matter of changing last names. The only legal category for the stranger's child was some form of indenture: In other words, they could only become part of a houschold as an employee.

The fuzziness was intentional, largely because English common law, the basis for the American system, simply ignored the possibility of adoption. The landed gentry were emphatically uninterested in last-minute intrusions from illegitimate heirs waving legal papers. In the colonial era and up through the early nineteenth century, Americans left the adoption question unanswered because there was no need to answer it. They were used to children coming and going, sometimes as apprentices, sometimes as servants.

The close-knit colonial towns and extended households of the seventeenth and eighteenth centuries grew into cities in the nineteenth century, the old neighborhoods filling up with newcomers, foreigners with strange accents and startlingly different customs. Population growth gave many Americans both the freedom and the burden of anonymity; you could pass the day without seeing the same person twice. But that spelled trouble for many children, especially those in need of a good home.

Take the case of Hannah Flovell, who we met in the previous chapter. Thoroughly fed up with the girl's lying aunt and unstable mother, the orphanage managers decided to place her in a suitable household. The first situation looked promising, an indenture to the wealthy widow of a former Massachusetts governor. But it did not last. Before long, the erstwhile Lady Bountiful sent Hannah packing back to the orphanage, complaining of her "troublesome" behavior. When the managers refused to void the indenture contact, the woman took matters into her own hands and shipped the hapless Hannah off to the home of a friend. That situation turned out to be so abusive that the child left on her own and attached herself to another family. Now no one was happy. Poor little Hannah went back to the orphanage until all the parties agreed that she could return to her last home as an indentured servant. It is to the credit of none of the adults involved that somehow, according to orphanage records, the serially unwanted child ended up a "good and useful girl."[1]

The Massachusetts law, which served as a model for other states, sorted through the confusion—kind of. It made clear that the orphan came into the home not as a laborer or an indentured servant but as a son or a daughter, exactly and only that. But the law also added a new layer of murkiness. It was now up to a judge to determine whether the prospective parents were "of sufficient ability to bring up the child, and furnish suitable nurture and education"—in other words, whether they were worthy.[2] We are still working on figuring out that one. At the time, though, the legal solution looked solid, even a little bit patriotic. Adoption was democracy in action, a direct rebuke to Old World anxieties about aristocracies and bloodlines and opening all kinds of new possibilities for homeless children and childless families.

So far, so good. To a sentimental Victorian, nothing evoked more pathos than a motherless child finding a warm, loving home—just ask Oliver Twist and David Copperfield. No one worried (yet) that adopted children would grow up odd or abnormal, nor did they stigmatize adoptive parents as overly needy or psychologically damaged. Nobody talked about "real" families and adoptive ones. How did we get from that idealistic starting point to the present day, where adoption has become so rare and so difficult, involving far more than just a name change and a safe, comfortable home?

We are simply awkward around adoption, never sure about what questions to ask or what to assume. I know this by experience, in fact. When we adopted our son Nate, it was through a semi-open process, a new practice at the time. Everyone's identities remained private, but we received a lot of background information about Nate's birth parents, and they had the option to open the files when he reached eighteen. Even so, we were in uncharted territory. One day, I was wheeling Nate around the neighborhood in a baby carriage, and a man stopped to admire him. "Wow, he's a healthy kid," he said. "His father must be pretty big." Without thinking, I replied that I didn't really know for sure—and then realized, as he smiled back at me with polite confusion, that I should probably come up with a better answer.

It wasn't entirely my fault though. Behind the mixed signals I was giving off was an unspoken social convention, an assumption that Nathan had to be my biological son. It didn't occur to the man that I, a young professional-looking white woman, was walking around with someone else's baby. In fact, in the moment, the easiest explanation was that I was scandalously loose and shockingly forgetful.

Chalk it up to our paltry modern imagination. In another time or place, the kindly gentleman peering into my baby carriage would have considered a variety of legitimate explanations for my relationship with Nate.

Blame the twentieth century. For the last hundred years or so, adoption has become tangled up with some of the most difficult and divisive questions of the modern era, from the definition of a family to the right to privacy to the proper way to raise a child. And let's not forget the host of other hot-button issues associated with adoption: race and single parenting, the legal rights of same-sex households, and, of course, the brave new world of reproductive technologies. Despite a long human history of people parenting other people's children, adoption has taken on an aura of risk. Even in a society moving toward tolerance for all kinds of diversity, we still cling to the notion that blood is always thicker than water, that biological ties between parents and children are the most natural, the most important, and the safest.

So how did we get here?

ANOTHER ADOPTION STORY

"We were in Paris and the month was May." This particular tale, published in the *Woman's Home Companion* in 1916, opens with a childless American couple mired in a delicate sadness. Though surrounded by "flowers and gayety and joyous Parisian sunshine," they are despondent, resigning themselves to an empty cradle and dull days ahead. Decades earlier, they would have searched for an orphan—the husband can still remember how, when he was a boy, the local orphanage dispatched a load of candidates to the Sunday morning church service, marching them down the aisle two by two. But times have changed; the orphanage is gone and, with it, the traditional source of adoptable children.[3]

Adoption was, in fact, frowned upon in 1916. As we saw in the last chapter, do-gooders had spent the last part of the nineteenth century removing children from unfit homes, even to the point of piling them onto trains headed to unknown destinations in the Midwest. But by the time our couple goes to Paris, the conventional wisdom has reversed itself. The best thing for all concerned, child welfare professionals agreed, was to keep the family together, even when it was clearly dysfunctional. Bad parents needed the "civilizing influence" their children provided. A good dose of parental responsibility, it was believed, would keep them on the straight and narrow.[4] Even a bad family was thought to be better than a soulless institution. By the early twentieth century, orphanages, orphan trains, and baby farmers were becoming—mercifully in most cases—a thing of the past. Families needed to stay together at all costs. Adoption, as one child welfare expert put it, was the worst possible outcome, tantamount to "abortion after birth."[5]

Our story of the beautifully sad couple in Paris, however, is a fairy tale, and so, in short order, they find a perfect baby boy in a French orphanage. After a short heart-pounding interlude, a Parisian judge approves the adoption, and the three travel to the United States as a family. The little European orphan goes on to live a charmed American life, the much-beloved son of wealthy, well-educated parents.

"Except for just one thing," the adoptive father admits. People around them are acting strangely, worrying in whispers about the lack of blood ties, warning that "you can never truly love a child unless the child is your own by birth." Has the couple really considered the risks involved?

Perhaps their beautiful French baby is the offspring of French criminals or, even worse, intellectual dullards. Perhaps they spawned a youngster incapable of following in the footsteps of his successful adoptive father. Remember that this was an era fascinated by the burgeoning new science of genetics—and deeply worried about its social implications. Decades before the Third Reich took the theory of eugenics to its tragic conclusion, many Americans were speculating openly about "bad blood" and "race suicide," and passing those concerns on to adoptive families. (We will return to this subject in the next chapter.)

In our story, nurture easily prevails over nature. The little boy proves so pleasing that, before long, the couple begins to consider, as the father puts it, "risking another venture." This time, however, with no French orphanages to search, they turn to—yes—the want ads in their local newspaper. Here's yet another case of behavior once considered socially acceptable seeming downright deplorable today. And, in this case, it was. Horror stories proliferated about unscrupulous medical professionals literally selling the children of unwed mothers. ("I gave 25 cents and a canary bird for it," one such maternal nightmare gloated.[6]) It all just looked too transactional. And it was truly awful. Childless couples scanning newspaper advertisements could and did stipulate eye and hair color, even certain levels of intelligence; they could send back a child who failed to meet their expectations.[7]

The couple in our story comes across an advertisement for the perfect addition to their family, a blue-eyed baby girl in need of a home. But, as fate would have it, a surprise pregnancy intervenes. Yet even this good news renders the couple's perpetually unsupportive family and friends more dubious than ever. They are certain the new baby will provide more proof that their first child was a tragic mistake.

This time, the couple will realize that they are "the victims of a huge, huge joke," and see "what a hollow, insipid, sham substitute for parenthood adoption really was."

They decide that none of it matters. "For weeks, I journeyed back and forth between the house and the hospital," the father recalls. "I would kiss the soft, warm little forehead of the son that had been born to us, then go home and be welcomed with mad outbursts of affection by the son we had adopted. Could I discover any difference in our love for those two? Could their mother? Could anybody looking on? Impossible!" Adoption ends up an incidental detail in this family's story, an inconsequential bump in the road—at least as it was related to the readers of *Woman's Home Companion*. But the story also illustrates how, by the early twentieth century, the old practice of trusting children to the care of unrelated adults was making a lot of people very uncomfortable.

The solution was to create strict guidelines for adoption, what historian Ellen Herman calls "kinship by design."[8] In the twentieth century, and on into our own times, adoption was made safe through careful professional oversight. Randomness and risk were dispatched along with baby farms, orphanages, and shady newspaper advertisements. In their place, a cohort of trained social workers took note of ethnicity, color of hair and eyes, and body type, and even made guesses about the child's intellectual potential. The goal was to create a seamless pairing between parents and baby, a perfect physical and psychological match.

Perfection was not going to be easy, however. The first set of Minimum Safeguards in Adoption, issued in 1938, stipulated that adoptees were owed not just education and loving care but also "the feeling of security to which any child is entitled."[9] In a similar way, the adoptive parents deserved a measure of certainty, the knowledge that their little bundle of joy had been screened to meet their "reasonable expectations."[10] Together they would create what social work professionals declared was a "normal family group."[11]

Normal is an interesting word, of course, especially when juxtaposed with *family*. A hundred years ago, child welfare professionals believed they had the tools to determine whether prospective parents measured up—and what they should be measuring up to. They set out, as Herman puts it, dead certain that they could locate "emotionally healthy couples in a sea of maladjusted marriages."[12] But what in the world did that mean? A hundred years ago, social work manuals came with a set of boxes to tick, mandating a thorough inspection of everything in sight, from the home's "general cleanliness" to the potential mother's cooking and baking skills. No certified professional would place a child in a home without good heating and plumbing, not to mention refrigeration, ventilation, and an adequate water supply.[13] In other words, struggling artists or single women in apartments need not apply: "Normal" meant a married heterosexual, financially responsible, middle-class couple with solid churchgoing credentials, traditional in every respect, except their inability to conceive a child.

But even that single flaw raised suspicion. What if that waiting couple, with their well-ventilated house and perfectly positioned throw pillows, was hiding some deep psychological secret? As we have seen, by the mid-twentieth century, some of the nation's leading medical professionals were willing to suspect that childlessness was more a psychological than a physical problem. Viola Bernard, who taught the psychosocial dynamics of reproduction at Columbia Medical School, warned that an infertile couple might actually be harboring an unconscious hostility toward parenthood, a defect, she said, that was clearly "ominous for children."[14] The adoption process thus became a therapeutic opportunity, a chance for agency social workers to help prospective parents work through what were undoubtedly tangled reasons for seeking an adoption. Or else. Any lack of cooperation, any degree of hesitation pushed the couple down the waiting list, maybe even eliminating them from the running altogether.[15]

The potential adoptive mother fell under special scrutiny. According to a set of standards issued in 1958, "acceptance of sex roles" was a sign of a woman's "emotional maturity." Career types, in other words, need not apply—and apparently they did not. A 1957 study of some sixty adoption agencies found only two applicants who said they were planning to stay in the workforce.[16]

The final ingredient in this unstable psychological stew was secrecy, a subject we will take up more fully in a later chapter. But for the moment, we can agree that post–World War II American culture was not an easy place for unwed parents. Before then, no one much bothered to hide a child's backstory—in many cases adoptees were old enough to know their own origins—nor did they block access to original birth certificates or court records.[17] In the baby booming 1950s and 1960s, when adoption rates surged, the typical adoptee was an infant, born out of wedlock. That meant that secrecy was not just possible but desirable.[18]

If postwar society was dubious about adoptive mothers, it was openly judgmental of their unwed counterparts. No longer objects of pity, "ruined" by predatory and unscrupulous men, the so-called fallen women of the twentieth century were at best pathetic, knowingly or foolishly getting themselves into "trouble." The popular psychology of the postwar era viewed them as fundamentally flawed, perhaps even infantile, allowing themselves to become pregnant in order to capture and keep a male caretaker. Unwed mothers, said Edmund Pollock of New York University, suffered from a penis envy "so profound that it could only be expressed in having a child."[19] Or worse, an unwed mother was bent on self-harm, using her reproductive organs, as one therapist speculated, "as the tool with which to hurt herself."[20] In the era before *Roe v. Wade*, the solution deemed best for all concerned was hiding the pregnancy and sending the girl off to bide her time in a maternity home. Redemption came once she had given birth and relinquished the baby, after which she would return home and pick up where she left off, chastened and cleansed.

No wonder we are still worrying about adoption. This less-than-optimal psychological scenario, what one author calls a "vast exercise in social engineering, unlike any other in American history,"[21] continues to define our perceptions: We still see adoption as a toxic mix of secrecy and shame, topped off by a big helping of white middle-class normality. That does not mean, of course, that the actual experience matches the public perception. Certainly in thousands of adoptive homes, love and patience triumph over perfectionism—in fact, if my extended family is any indication, the challenge brings out the best in everybody, and they enfold their adopted cousins with extraordinary warmth and acceptance.

The new ethic in twenty-first-century adoption is honesty. We have largely abandoned the old practice of matching families, largely because it makes logical sense to do so. Today about 40 percent of adopted children come from different racial and cultural backgrounds than their adoptive parents.[22] As we've seen, the typical adoptee is not white but is instead mixed-race, international, often older, or perhaps coming out of the foster care system. The typical adoptive parents are no longer middle-to-upper-middle-class white couples but same-sex couples, single women (and sometimes men), or relatives taking in an older child. Though laws vary state to state, the majority of adoptions are open, with both sets of parents known to each other. In many ways, late twentieth-century adoptions were a return to an earlier set of practices, echoing the law passed by the Massachusetts legislature in 1851, creating families that were non-biological but legally "real." No more perfect pairings, no more subterfuge.

Yet, even in this new day, old prejudices persist. Adoption just feels unsettling. After all, aren't families supposed to have some kind of internal logic, some larger explanation for why that particular group of people exists together? I used to wonder that too.

NO MORE MATCHING

"Mom, you are so *white*." At seven, Anna had a knack for declaring both the obvious and the unsayable. But this time I did not hedge. "Yes," I told her, "I really, really am, no question. If you have any doubts, just watch me try to clap to music on the offbeat." In contrast to my pale Dutch build, she was brown and solid, her hair thick and black. I had learned to manage life from the neck up, but she lived on an emotional roller coaster, with peaks and plunges I could not begin to imagine.

We are, in other words, a typical adoptive family of our time and place, a human patchwork of races and ethnicities, personalities and preferences. We definitely do not match. So—and here are the questions Anna was trying to ask me: What do we do with those differences? What then are we?

The big conversation in adoption circles, since the late 1960s and 1970s, has been about race and ethnicity. Beginning back then, increasing numbers of African American children, who had been long ignored by adoption agencies and left to the uncertain prospects of the foster care system, were being placed into homes with white parents. Transracial adoption was a new kind of social engineering, of course, based on a different idealistic vision that certainly took some boldness, if not bravery, to implement. Against a background of race riots and segregationist violence, mixed-race families created by adoption would demonstrate the power of love and understanding, the belief that the "content of character" mattered far more than the accident of skin color.

Not everyone believed in this idealistic social vision, however. In 1972, the National Association of Black Social Workers came out in direct opposition to interracial adoptions. NABSW president William T. Merritt was explicit: "Black children belong physically, psychologically and culturally in black families." Even the best-intentioned white parents, he said, were complicit in a "form of genocide." All the love in the world could not change reality: Black children growing up in a racist society needed Black parents. Only they could provide a cultural identity and, even more important, prepare them for the complicated challenges that lay ahead.[23]

By then, however, interracial and international adoptions already had a history, albeit a complicated one. Beginning in the 1950s, singing star Josephine Baker put together what she called her "rainbow tribe," twelve children adopted from all over the world. History knows Baker as the dazzling and risqué performer who enchanted European audiences in the post–World War I era. Never one to miss an adventure, during World War II, she spied for the French Resistance and both US and British intelligence. In the postwar years, she joined the civil rights movement—during her career, Baker endured repeated harassment and affront because of American segregation laws—and decided to build an unconventional family. Baker's children came from Japan, Venezuela, France, Belgium, and Finland, and they lived with her at Les Milandes, an estate with a hotel, a jazz club, a miniature golf course, and a wax museum detailing Baker's life. But this was no ordinary celebrity adoption, the kind we are used to seeing from megastars like Madonna and Angelina Jolie. Baker never demanded privacy or tried to pretend that racial differences were trivial. She had her children on full display, entertaining visitors with songs and playing in a courtyard in full view of an awestruck public, as a visual argument for human equality.[24]

So much about Baker's rainbow tribe seems hard to understand today. She arbitrarily changed her children's names and in some cases selected their religious faiths in order to better show how our common humanity could overcome all difference. But she was certainly not alone in her racial idealism, especially in the case of international adoptions.

The background here was war and foreign policy, the thousands upon thousands of orphans left by conflicts in Korea, Vietnam, and across Asia. Here the pioneer in international adoptions was the writer Pearl Buck, who founded Welcome House in 1949 to take in mixed-race "Amerasian" children (a term she coined) who had been abandoned by their American GI fathers and ostracized by racial prejudice in their own societies, left to survive on the streets and in orphanages. Buck not only championed these marginalized children but took them into her own family, adopting seven children, including two with African fathers. She insisted that skin color meant nothing. Whatever prejudices her children might meet in the outside world "they could cope with because at home there was only love and acceptance."[25]

The other inspiration for adopting across international and cultural borders was Helen Doss, who published the bestseller *The Family Nobody Wanted* in 1954. She and her husband adopted twelve children of color from all over the world: Indian, Filipino, Balinese, Malayan, Mexican, and Native American. Her book, later a movie starring Shirley Jones of *Partridge Family* fame, was a super-charged affirmation of the postwar nuclear family and its power to transcend every kind of racial difference. Doss, like Buck, insisted that skin color was irrelevant to children raised in loving, affirmative homes. When her blond, blue-eyed biological son played cowboys and Indians with his adopted Indian brother, the two switched roles without a moment's hesitation. She countered critics with ebullient good humor and an insistence that her family was no less "real" than a biological one, underscoring the point with the title of her 1959 book, a story of two girls adopted from Hawaii, *The Really Real Family*.

But did it work? Was love and acceptance really enough? Early on, the evidence suggested yes: Color differences did not matter. The evidence came from studies conducted in the 1970s and 1980s, finding little racial friction in mixed-race families and, more important, positive racial attitudes among the children. White parents seemed to be succeeding in raising Black children, after all. The adoptees were thriving, proud of their racial identities and abounding in self-esteem. Researchers happily concluded that color blindness was a winning strategy for white parents. Ignoring differences actually worked.

These were the early days though. The adoptees were still young, not yet out in the world and subject to the full force of racial stereotyping. "As I got older, I stopped being this cute little boy," one young man explained, "and others perceived me as this black teenager and a menace to society. Apparently, I was liable to rape, kill, or whatever. I got pulled over by the cops. I got slammed against the wall with a flashlight in my face." Not surprisingly, later studies of Black adoptees were not as sunny as the first. Black sociologist and adoptee Rhonda Roorda has recorded many personal stories of "shock, deep loneliness, low self-worth, emotional trauma, a desire to belong, and a desperate need for healing and direction." The information that those children needed, about growing up and living as Black people in a racist society, she writes, simply "did not exist in the white world."[26]

Love and understanding are important, but are they enough? Can they alone counter the psychological toll on children who grow up in a setting where race is deemed unimportant and then find out that, in the wider world, it matters a great deal? What happens to children who are unprepared for life in a racist society, where they will learn to live as Black or Asian or Latino adults?

There are no rules, no neat sets of procedures for families who cross thick social boundaries. At the very least, interracial families, parents especially, need a special degree of self-awareness and personal flexibility. Roorda and others encourage parents to seek outside support, to locate places where their children will find non-white friends and trusted mentors of their own race. It's important to be intentional, to venture sometimes far from racial comfort zones, for the sake of adopted children, and to accept the fact that a transracial adoption will bring changes impossible to know in advance. "I compare it to a poetry-jazz improvisation of unique and colorful sounds," says Roorda, "all playing significant parts that rely on each other but ultimately transform each other."[27]

Helen Doss certainly helped shape my racial attitudes. Like many a suburban preteen, I had read *The Family Nobody Wanted* and was ready to believe in the power of love and acceptance. For a long time, I had no reason to think otherwise: I knew families with Korean adoptees and went to a Christian summer camp where I made friends with my Black and Latina cabinmates from inner-city Newark.

But I also had an inkling that the problem was bigger than switching roles in cowboys and Indians. As a mildly rebellious, bookish high school student in the 1970s, my personal reading list included *The Autobiography of Malcolm X*, Eldridge Cleaver's *Soul on Ice*, and Richard Wright's *Native Son*. Graduate school brought me to Baltimore and Washington, DC, where, for the first time, I rode the bus and shopped for groceries as a white person, a racial minority in a predominantly Black city. And I kept reading. Decades before anyone worried about critical race theory, my doctoral program in American history included hair-raising scholarship about the realities of slavery and its present-day legacy. I was educated enough, in other words, to know some of what I did not—could not—otherwise know about race and racism.

When we first contacted an adoption agency in the early 1980s, we assumed our child would not look like us. Given the availability of birth control and abortion, and the stigma removed from unwed pregnancies, a white infant was a nonstarter. The wait for a white baby could take years—a lifetime for someone approaching thirty. We did not hesitate to tell the agency we were open to pretty much any child. It's fair to say that we began the adoption process in a practical frame of mind but also, I should add, equipped with some hard-won self-knowledge. All those years of infertility treatments were humbling, a monthly reminder that the universe did not revolve around our personal priorities. And perhaps because of that moral recalibration, we were not interested in finding a tiny replica of ourselves, a replacement for the child we had not managed to conceive. Whoever came into our home would be, and had to be, different. In the end, we simply wanted a child, and above all, a child who needed us.

What we didn't know was how much we still had left to learn.

SECRETS AND TRUTH

Anna and I looked different from each other, and, we would discover, the world treated us accordingly. It helped, at least for a while, that we lived in the heart of Cambridge, Massachusetts, a city where diversity was not just celebrated but sought. The public schools were a montage of races and colors and sexualities, and, most important for us, included many multiracial adoptive families. Back in the 1980s and 1990s, before it was more widely acceptable, Cambridge was also a safe space for households with two dads or two moms, many of whom were raising adopted children. In that little corner of the world, our unmatched family was far from exceptional—the unconventional was almost a little bit normal.

But not for long. This time Anna did not say it out loud, but I knew for a fact that I was very, very white one evening when she and I were walking through downtown Chicago, looking for a place to eat. By then, the little cross-eyed baby had grown into a beautiful young woman with long black hair and a graceful heart-shaped face—all of which were a magnet for male admiration. It was a little late to be out in a strange city, but the streets were busy, and there were plenty of people on the sidewalks, which I, considering myself a fairly experienced urbanite, took as a sign of safety.

And then I saw how little I knew. Apparently, every man we encountered had something to say, an invitation or a muttered comment. It became clear that all those random men were assuming that my daughter was, for lack of a better word, available. The reason was not our age difference, or even our comparative physical attractiveness—it was the color of our skin. Matthew Pratt Guterl, who has written a beautifully perceptive account of growing up as a white biological child in a multiracial adoptive family, says this awareness of unfathomable social distance is often "just at the edge of perception." He saw in his siblings a "meaningful Black interiority shared between them, away from the spotlight, off stage, in a place where my eyes cannot—and should not—easily see. I remember that my eyes are not mine alone, and that I bring whiteness with me where I go, and to whatever I see."[28]

I had been let in on a secret: The child I had learned to love as my own was, to the outside world, someone else, a person defined by the color of her skin. The two of us stood on either side of a social gulf we could not close.

Yet we are still family. Of course, by the simplest definition, the sharing of genetic material, we are not and never will be. In a similar way, the social apparatus we have constructed around skin color denies us "authentic" relationships. We will not, by love or force of will, overcome racial prejudice or centuries of injustice—individual acts are meaningful, but there's no denying the social realities that surround us. Systems matter.

But we do have some say in what social rules we follow, and I suggest that race does not always have to have the final word. There are other ways for adoptive parents and children to understand why they are a family. Though my household might have been created in the most random of ways, at the professionally trained whim of a social worker, there is nothing arbitrary about our life together. Because we have no biological fallback, we recommit to each other over and over. We are a family on purpose.

We are, in other words, kin.

BELONGING

Anna's daughter turned one at a family reunion on Cape Cod. As we sat around the dinner table, united in our adoration of the little one methodically smearing birthday cake into her hair, I made a mental tally: Not a single person there was related to me by blood. Most of them weren't related to each other either. Only three people in that gathering were genetically connected to my granddaughter Éva: my daughter Anna, her husband Tamas, and his mother, who had flown in from Budapest. Other than that, we were a random assortment of adults, most of us brought together by legal rather than biological auspices, all celebrating a beloved person and a beloved event.

Kin is an antique-sounding word, but it's far more expansive and flexible than *family*, which, by long custom in modern Western culture, we understand only in a biological sense. Americans believe that "blood" is natural. It's not just a substance, a thing, but a particular kind of relationship that, unlike marriage or stepparenting, can't be terminated—no matter how much some of us might wish it. If we widen our perspective a bit, if we go beyond our particular time and place and our beliefs about what constitutes a "real" relationship, we can begin to see the variety and complexity of family bonds across time and geography—the power of kinship.

In some Malaysian societies, for example, kinship is not some fixed genetic identity but a "process of becoming," as anthropologist Janet Carsten describes it.[29] People are related not through a one-time event or because they share a particular genetic code but through ritual and relationships that grow and evolve across lifetimes. Kinship is almost literally more about nurture than nature: Mothers, children, and siblings become kin to each other when they eat rice cooked over the same hearth. There are even exceptions to the "doctrine of single paternity," the belief that every child has only one father. Some Amazonian cultures, writes social scientist and physician Nicholas Christakis, believe that intercourse should continue throughout a pregnancy, and each of the woman's partners is considered a father of the child. On the other end of the spectrum, the Na people in Tibet believe that men merely "water" a baby already inside a woman's womb, and "it makes no difference who does the watering."[30]

Our Western notion, that a child is either biological or adopted, one or the other and nothing else, is a minority view. The Baatombu in Northern Benin, for example, do not distinguish between birth and foster parents. In fact, they think that children fare best with nonrelatives, who are more likely to treat them fairly and discipline the most consistently. And at bottom, the Baatombu give young children a lot more credit than we do. They do not worry that moving a child from one home to another will damage them for life.[31]

Modern Western people are, in other words, WEIRD. That's the acronym created by Harvard anthropologist Joseph Henrich to describe what most of us assume is normal:

Western, educated, industrialized, rich, and democratic. It means, among other things, that we believe in the necessity of fostering individual self-esteem as the key to a satisfying life, or as Henrich describes it, "the successful cultivation of a set of unique personal attributes that capture one's 'true self.'" Or consider this: We believe that what matters most is what we carry inside. The essential "you" is a function of your personality, your convictions, perhaps some bits of accumulated knowledge. It is not what happens on the outside, in families and community relationships. These are, if anything, an impediment to what we believe is a good life, standing up for yourself and becoming an independent, self-actualized adult. This is in contrast to non-WEIRD societies, in which well-being is other-directed. In these societies, your sense of rightness depends on how you cooperate, how you operate as a member of a group.[32]

Henrich also points out that the kinship rules that are taken for granted in Western societies are abnormal almost everywhere else. We trace our line of descent through both parents, not just one, and we squirm over cousins marrying each other. We believe that the most normal families have one husband and one wife, and include only the children from that relationship, not any random relative who happens to wander in. We believe it is normal for newly married couples to move out and set up a separate household.

These traits are not just WEIRD but also extremely rare among cultures worldwide. Over half the societies described in the Ethnographic Atlas, an anthropological database of some 1,200 groups around the world, have exactly none of those characteristics. Only 0.7 percent of those listed in the atlas possess all five. In other words, says Henrich, 99.3 percent of societies in a global database are different from what modern Western people consider not just normal, but the best and the most "human" way to live.[33]

Our assumptions about nuclear families are even stranger if we look across the span of human history. If we imagine the past 1.8 million years as a movie of a hundred minutes, says anthropologist David Samson, author of *Our Tribal Future*, then hunter-gatherers only appear after an hour has gone by. At eighty-four minutes, tribes form, and at ninety-nine minutes, *Homo sapiens* triumph over their Neanderthal rivals. Human civilization happens in the last thirty seconds of the film, and writing happens after another fifteen seconds elapse. The nuclear family, says Samson, comes into being in the last five seconds of our hundred-minute movie, the blink of an eye in the history of humanity.[34]

There's plenty of evidence that many Americans today wouldn't mind some of the old ways, that they both need and want wider, richer family ties. For a lot of practical reasons, the two-parent nuclear family has become a fantasy lifestyle for more and more of us, unattainable in these times of impossible housing prices, student debt, and the often crippling costs of old age. The journalist David Brooks points out that only a third of Americans now live in such homes, and they tend to be the people who can afford that level of independence, with the financial resources to pay for childcare, the mortgage on a single family home, and the extracurricular activities for their children that will brighten applications to a college or university. If anything, says Brooks, those kinds of families are making things worse for the rest, widening their basic privilege into a permanent advantage.

Yet, in other ways, the rest of us, who have to rely on aunts and uncles, grandparents and neighbors, are so much better off. We are rediscovering a forgotten truth of human history, that bigger and more diverse families are good for people. Yes, having Aunt Charlotte hanging around the kitchen to critique your cooking skills might not be fun, but she can also take your fourteen-year-old out for ice cream when youthful hormones have become too much for you to handle. Extended kin can act as "shock absorbers," as Brooks says. When personalities clash, or someone becomes sick or incapacitated, deputy parents provide resilient, flexible bonds that every human relationship requires.[35]

This kind of ongoing commitment is something more, I think, than the idea of "families we choose." That's a wonderful description of households who do not fit the two-parent, married, two-generational ideal, formed by same-sex partnerships, friendships, or a whole variety of blended relationships. But I don't think the phrase adequately captures the day-to-day reality. "Choosing" suggests a one-time decision, but life with other human beings is a long string of choices, made repeatedly, over days and months and years and decades. I don't say the angry words I'm thinking, or I do a chore that technically is not my responsibility; I sit with someone who is ill when I'd rather be on my bicycle, and I listen to my mother's umpteenth reprisal of a story I've already heard a million times and act as surprised as if it were the first time.

Kin, after all, is the root of *kindness*, a word with little to no association with biology or genetics. In the Hebrew scriptures, it is love for the stranger, compassion and care for the outsider, the foreigner. The scope of kindness is endless in fact. St. Isaac of Syria, a seventh-century mystic, calls on us to "burn with love for the whole of creation: for humankind, for the birds, for the beasts, for every creature." It's possible to care, to feel an intense relationship with all kinds of people, maybe even an animal or two, beyond your small nuclear family.[36]

Why is this all so difficult? It's not just that the benchmark for successful parenting is your children leaving home and never coming back. And it's not just our belief that every family should have the money, social connections, and emotional resources to survive on its own. American capitalism and its discontents are certainly part of this picture, but not its entirety. I think the answer goes back to the kinds of relationships we consider "real"—and those that we reject as presumably "unreal." Perhaps I bring a particular sensitivity here, after years of comments about my children's "real" parents, the clear assumption that what is biological is true, and anything other than that, i.e., my claims to motherhood, are thin and suspect. But plenty of other people, including millions beyond the confines of our modern time and place, would agree with me.

We are so used to the idea that "authenticity" is a personal quest, the separate soul's journey to its own true reality. "Not only should I not fit my life to the demands of external conformity," writes philosopher Charles Taylor; "I can't even find the model to live by outside myself. I can only find it within."[37] Our cultural heroes possess a sense of self that is unique, singular, original, and complete; they have a particular kind of courage, allowing them to strip down to the absolute essentials, like David Thoreau in his mythical solitude on Walden Pond. Friends and family and assorted role models can help with the quest, but they are not, by definition, part of it. Thus, the Disney princess must leave her demanding parents, the cowboy has to ride off in search of open space and freedom, and political zealots must pursue absolute purity beyond the reach of "fake" news and party loyalties. The spiritual seeker finds God outside the company of others, especially those who impose religious rules and demand rituals. Our impulse is to pare down and pare down and pare down, until we have validated only the most essential, the most personal kinds of relationships.

We are, in fact, at the end of a long historical process, one in which fashioning a self has become not just possible but mandatory. "It is what we, as human beings, are *for*," writes historian Tara Isabella Burton. "We are creators of ourselves, of our lives, of the world around us." Her survey of expressive individualism, beginning with Renaissance figures like Leonardo da Vinci and ending with Kim Kardashian, demonstrates the power of this assumption, that "our personal desires are the truest, deepest parts of ourselves and should dictate our lives and our fates."[38]

I understand the urge. Surrounded as we are by algorithms and influencers, gaslighters and bamboozlers, independent thinking is not just a lifestyle choice—it's a critical tool for survival. For so many people growing up today, that metaphorical room of one's own, a place to think and decide and become beyond the reach of social media is an absolute mental health necessity.

But at some point, we need to find a way back in. In this era of bamboozlement, none of us are going to come near the truth on our own. The more fundamental truth, deeper than anything you might write in a journal or discover on a therapist's couch, is that other people matter. They have created you. They make you real. Thus, in the Malaysian society that Janet Carsten studied, when people ask about each other's families, they say, "How many siblings *are* you?" not "How many siblings do you have?"[39] As one of six children, I understand that sentiment well. I am myself but also the person my family made me. Even now, hundreds of miles distant from my five siblings, I am myself minus the rough edges they knocked off, the reality checks they administered, but I am also filled out by the jokes we shared, the stories we told each other when we thought our parents were not listening.

So many other people, before and beyond our modern world, already know this. Before there were journals and diaries, one-person plays and best-selling autobiographies, personal identity was a group project. When Socrates issued the dictum to "know thyself," he was not ordering his disciples to self-actualize. "To know yourself," writes the philosopher Charles Guignon, "…is to know above all what your *place* is in the scheme of things—what you are and what you should be as that has been laid out in advance by the cosmic order."[40]

My mixed and mixed-up family—and any family, biological or single-parent or same-sex or blended or something more—is "real" when the members stay in conversation with each other. It becomes authentic when there is reconciliation after a wrong, understanding after a failure. It also happens when I realize that the other's life experience is solely theirs and allow it to remain incomprehensible to me. Without a doubt, the task of creating and maintaining an authentic self requires solitude and separation—the demands of modernity are far more shrill and demanding than our ancestors could have ever imagined. But at the end, we all need to return and locate ourselves in the wider scheme of things. An authentic life requires us to roll out the map, find the spot that marks "you are here," and then contemplate all that lies beyond in the incredibly vast and diverse world we inhabit together.

CHAPTER 4

FATE

After the evening rush hour, when all the suburban commuters are safely at home, Boston's Orange Line becomes unpredictable. The trains trundling past gritty backlots and rundown factories carry a random assortment of passengers, each one of them, I like to imagine, with a story to tell. Some of the less fortunate are bedding down for a few hours of sleep, surrounded by plastic bags full of recyclables. Others have already nodded off, obviously coming home after long hours at a demanding job or a late-night class. Bunker Hill Community College, one of the Orange Line's popular stops, was operating almost twenty-four seven before the pandemic turned education online. Still others are wide awake and making sure the rest of us are too, carrying on energetic conversations into cell phones, most of them in languages not taught in the average American high school.

I'm enough of a public transportation veteran to know that I should mind my own business. During my many years riding the Orange Line to work in Boston, I have been yelled at by strangers, hit up for money, and forced into long and crazy conversations. I have learned to avoid direct eye contact.

Then there was that one night. I glanced across the aisle and saw a young Vietnamese man, his arms folded across his chest, deep in thought. I stared, unable to look away. That young man was a dead ringer for my adopted son. To this day, I don't know what startled me most. Perhaps it was the tilt of his head, the arc of his body, or an inward expression that had become as familiar to me as my own face. Years later, I still wonder whether, in that random moment, I had come across one of Nathan's biological relatives, a member of his extended Vietnamese family.

Nate was certainly full of surprises. In grade school, he became enamored of ramen noodles, and in characteristic fashion, cooked them with meticulous precision. He measured out the exact amount of water required for the broth and watched the timer to make sure he turned off the stove at the exact right moment. After a few scalding hot spills on our living room couch, he took to eating the noodles from a large glass serving bowl.

Then a pho restaurant opened in our neighborhood. I still remember the shock of recognition: noodles and broth in an enormous bowl, the size of a small washbasin. As my dining companion and I fumbled with our spoons and chopsticks, I had to wonder: Was Nathan's ramen ritual some ancestral memory springing to life, a genetic imperative to eat noodles and broth from a large glass bowl?

The idea seems ridiculous—and then you remember all of those stories about twins separated at birth. James Arthur Springer and James Edward Lewis were adopted by two different families, and each one was told that their twin had died at birth. When they finally met at age thirty-nine, the story was jaw-dropping. Each had married a woman named Linda, then divorced her and remarried a Betty. Each man had a son, one named James Allan and the other James Alan. Both had a dog named Toy when they were children. "This is really blowing our minds," said Springer. "It's weird. It's downright spooky."[1]

Indeed. Or take the case of Oskar Stőr and Jack Yule, identical twins separated when their parents divorced and then raised in diametrically opposite homes. Oskar grew up in Germany in the 1930s and became a member of the Hitler Youth movement. Jack stayed in Trinidad with his Jewish father and at age seventeen joined an Israeli kibbutz and then later served in Israel's military. Oskar was raised by women, Jack by men, into different religious faiths and vastly different politics. When the two met again at age twenty-one, at first it seemed there was not a lot to say—they needed a translator just to talk to each other—and then the coincidences began to pile up. Oskar and Jack liked the same foods, they spoke with the same cadence, asked the same questions. The two even shared odd nervous habits, like flushing the toilet both before and after using it.[2]

Then there's the story of Anna and her birth mother. Their first meeting—after many months of searching, with the help of a veteran social worker—took place in the parking lot of a truck stop off the Massachusetts Turnpike. Sara was on a trip north from her home in the South with her husband Jay, who drove a big rig. She'd just stepped out of the shower and was drying her hair with a towel when Anna pulled up.

Mother and daughter were back together after eighteen years apart, and clearly they had plenty to talk about. I don't know much about the specifics of the conversation that night—it wasn't my business, obviously—but I do know it changed everything. When I saw Anna later on that evening, there was no doubt about the transformation. She looked physically different, more settled perhaps, in sharper focus.

Clearly, there's something absolutely real and profound about knowing who you are and where you came from.

Sara and Jay came up to visit us in Cambridge that weekend, and for several years, we stayed in touch. Despite the vast social gulf between our families—they were ardent survivalists who issued a standing invitation to their Missouri bunker in the event of apocalypse—we had a lot in common. We all loved the same young woman.

The connection between Anna and Sara, across a gulf of life experiences, even personal tragedy, was undeniable. I heard it every time I talked to Sara on the phone, the same exact giggle as her biological daughter. It was identical, down to the last tiny lilted syllable.

How in the world did that happen? Did that unnerving echo begin in the womb, the adult Anna reproducing what she had heard as a fetus? Or maybe that giggle was a family trait, as spooky and unexplainable as those separated twins flushing the toilet before and after.

Maybe there's no need to keep debating the nature versus nurture question. Outward circumstances don't matter: Each one of us is simply living out a genetic destiny. Everything from your bathroom habits to the name of your childhood pet was fated from birth. Few of us, however, want to believe that. I am always a little amused at the astonishment of my academic peers, gifted people with Ivy League degrees and prestigious jobs, relating their progeny's latest achievement. "I can't believe that Junior is already reading at age two," says the tenured Harvard professor. We are less surprised: The child, like the parent, has won the genetic lottery. All that precociousness would manifest even if little Junior were raised in the forest by a pack of wolves.

Yet I also admit that, for an adoptive parent, all this talk of genetic destinies is a tad unnerving. There is no doubt that my children came with a set of inborn traits and tendencies, both physical and emotional. Now when I look at one of our first pictures of four-month-old Nathan, smiling knowingly at all the gears and levers in his Busy Box, I see the BMW technician he would become. He is who he was when we met him. Still, it is hard to believe that all my parenting was basically warehousing, that his life choices were simply the unfolding of the inevitable.

Clearly, genes matter. When Anna's little daughter Ếva was born, I saw, over and over, so much of what I was unable to see when Anna was a baby. My granddaughter's little moods and preferences, her rhythms of sleep and smiling, made perfect sense because I had seen them before. Yet when Anna was an infant, I had no such knowledge. She was a puzzle I often struggled to solve. Like Ếva, she was swift to anger as an infant, and as an inexperienced mother—and let's be honest, an adult who had been endowed by both nature and nurture with a more limited emotional range—I assumed the instantaneous rage was my fault, a defect in my mothering skills. I did not see that this was, as they say, a personality feature, not a glitch. Some people are just like that. Anna was an intensely observant baby, watchful to the point of wariness, an approach to life that I interpreted as insecurity, perhaps even an injury I had inflicted by adopting her. I could not know that she would always enter new situations this way and that the hesitation would later become a vulnerability.

An adoptee's child is such a miracle, the first chance to gaze into another face that looks like you, the first time to marvel over family resemblances. But that baby also comes with a sadness, the grandmother's realization of all the cues she missed, how much she did not—could not—understand.

Heredity is a mystery, and that makes it frustrating. We like mysteries solved in fifty minutes by a British detective—otherwise we get impatient. We want to know who is who and what is what, to measure and predict the balance of nature and nurture. At the same time, though, we should recognize that a lot of that discomfort is time-bound, even recent. It is in many ways specific to our time and place. And it is a big part of the reason we worry about adopting other people's children and our ancestors did not.

And so in this chapter, we consider another gulf we have crossed as modern people, the tangled and ancient debate about nature and nurture. It is a conversation that has changed radically over time in response to scientific discoveries and shifting social attitudes—and a major reason for the hesitancy around families formed by adoption rather than biology.

NATURE, NURTURE, AND EVERYTHING ELSE

For most of human history, people did not worry all that much about the relative importance of nature and nurture. There was, after all, no language for it. True, with the domestication of animals, herdsmen could see for a fact that spotted goats begat other spotted goats and brown cows begat more brown cows. Explaining why was more difficult, and so with the scientific tools many centuries off in the future, humanity resorted to what's still our default option, rampant speculation. After all, why would anyone assume a necessary connection between sex and pregnancy, two events that could occur weeks, perhaps months apart? Clearly, something was creating resemblances across generations—but what?

The answer had to be big. In a world inhabited by gods and goddesses, every corner thick with sacred meaning, it was not difficult to see every new life as a divine intervention. In the ancient world, each birth, whether people, plants, or animals, was a singular, miraculous event. Our modern idea of reproduction, in other words, would have made no sense in a prescientific world in which every newborn goat, stalk of sprouting wheat, or tiny human baby was thought to be *engendered*. This is a word that evokes creativity: We think of a musician fashioning a composition or an artist imagining the design for a mural on a wall, not the routine unfolding of a biological process.[3]

For centuries, no one asked for any more explanation than that. Nature and nurture were indistinguishable. And anyway, keeping track of family connections was really only a problem for rich people—the Romans' word *hereditas* had to do with recording and distributing money and property across generations. If peasants or shopkeepers noticed that father and son had the same color hair or the same oddly shaped nose, the coincidence was interesting but also explainable. They looked the same because of outside circumstances: They had both been conceived, born, and raised in the same climate, the same natural environment. Even with the slew of hereditary diseases and increasingly odd physical features that plagued ingrown European monarchies, no one felt the need to probe the mystery any further. Put all those family resemblances down to cold weather, a phase of the moon, or even the local geography. Tall people came from countries that were, according to Hippocrates, "level, windy, and well-watered," whereas short people predominated in "places that are low-lying, abounding in meadows and ill ventilated," with warm breezes and warm water.[4]

Given this abundantly loose connection between nature and nurture, we shouldn't be surprised that people had so few misgivings about raising other parents' children. Human beings were thought to be more malleable back then than they are now. Stocky little Claudius might have arrived looking like an outsider, but let him spend enough time battling chill winds in a mountain village, and his descendants would be as lanky and thin as everyone else there.

Our modern understanding of heredity required a shift in focus, the curious gaze turned downward, into the tiny worlds the first microscopes made visible. The results were startling. Imagine Anton von Leeuwenhoek in 1674 peering in wonder at the animalcules wriggling in the semen sample under his microscope, the Dutch and French scientists locked in competition, each racing to be the first to prove that the "female testicles" they had discovered in dogfish were in fact ovaries containing eggs.

We should pause and point out that this was not an immediate boost to womankind. The reigning theory, set forth by no less than Aristotle, was that females were basically receptacles for male sperm. Centuries would pass before anyone knew what those female testicles actually did. No one even saw a human egg until the early nineteenth century—and that, of course, raised yet more questions about what happened when egg and sperm came together.

Even then, we were still a long way from explaining how that union led to actual family resemblances. It would be a while before scientists truly understood the significance of Austrian monk Gregor Mendel's experiments with pea plants, demonstrating the mathematical laws behind the inheritance of dominant and latent traits across generations. The early science of heredity emerged after years of systematic recordkeeping and careful classifying by pioneers who were not dreamers or mystics but systematic, detail-oriented people with an eye to the long game—farmers, sheepherders, and monks. They were the ones who kept track of minute changes in pea plants and sheep, who kept decade after decade of records detailing diseases and disabilities in family genealogies. Progress required a certain bureaucratic imagination, in other words, belief in the ultimate value of the achingly mundane. In this sense, the concept of genetic inheritance is a thoroughly modern idea, made possible only within a predictable, disenchanted world, a universe governed by mathematical principles and fixed physical laws, "a force that expressed itself across the generations, altering the characters of individuals." The French called it *hérédité*, a word that did not appear in print in English until 1863.[5]

And even then, the mechanics were unclear. For all his brilliant theorizing about evolution, Charles Darwin could not say exactly how "latent" or "invisible" characteristics were transmitted from one generation to another. Darwin's cousin Francis Galton, the leading expert on all things hereditary, was keenly aware of all that scientists could not explain. Looking at egg cells through a microscope was, he said, like peering through a window into a post office and seeing the floor strewn with bags of mail, each one containing thousands of individual letters. Though the astute observer might "draw various valuable conclusions" about the postal system, said Galton, "they cannot read a single word of what the letters contain."[6]

Science did not eradicate mystery. Even when scientists realized that male sperm were not human beings in miniature or when they finally saw the union of egg and sperm in a Petri dish, they still had more questions than answers. They were a long way from explaining how two brown-eyed parents could produce a blue-eyed child or whether the offspring of Harvard professors would always learn to read by age two. Are a person's abilities and attitudes as heritable as the size of their feet? What's predetermined and what's a matter of choice?

In the modern era, as technology deepened our gaze into the infinitesimal, these were not, unfortunately, innocent questions.

BAD BLOOD

No one liked the Kallikak family, and for good reason. It wasn't just that they were dishonest, lazy, and ornery—they were also downright stupid. And, in fact, the problem was worse than that: The Kallikaks had been just plain bad for a long, long time, generations of terrible people marrying other terrible people and having terrible children.[7]

According to the best available genealogical evidence, the trouble started when Martin Kallikak, a Revolutionary War veteran, romanced a "feeble-minded" wench in a tavern and produced a feeble-minded son. From there, the Kallikaks went on to plague the human race with a flood of deviant offspring: alcoholics, prostitutes, criminals, and epileptics, each one more dimwitted than the last.[8]

By the early twentieth century, scientists believed they had a theory to explain it all. Henry Herbert Goddard was the reigning expert, director of the research laboratory at the Training School for Feeble-minded Girls and Boys in Vineland, New Jersey, and despite the name of that institution, a man of deeply humanitarian motives. The school was actually a pleasant, well-funded home for young people with a wide variety of intellectual disabilities, providing them both loving care and instruction in basic trades, in the hope that they would one day be self-supporting.[9]

There were exceptions, however, and that is where the Kallikaks come in. When the Vineland staff started working with eight-year-old Deborah Kallikak, she never got any better. Despite all their best efforts, the great-granddaughter of the original "Old Horror," Martin Kallikak, grew neither smarter nor more industrious. By the time she was a young woman, researchers were forced to conclude that all their efforts had come to nothing. It seems Deborah's fate was sealed that fateful day when Martin had encountered the willing tavern wench, many years ago.

Except that most of the story wasn't true. To begin with, the Kallikak family did not exist—this was a name researchers concocted (from the Greek for *horrible*) to preserve the real family's anonymity. Then it turns out that Old Horror was not simply the patriarch from hell—he also had forty-six "normal" descendants who had done nothing to deserve public opprobrium. To complicate matters further, the origin story of Martin and the tavern wench was also more legend than fact: The field researcher who traced the Kallikaks' genealogy had relied a fair bit on local yarns and hearsay evidence. There was no real evidence that the feeble-minded tavern wench was anything other than normally intelligent and of fine moral character. Most surprising to us today, none of the researchers stopped to wonder whether the criminality, abuse, and supposed stupidity they were witnessing had anything to do with the family's economic circumstances. No one considered whether decades of grinding poverty and rural isolation might have been not an effect but a cause of the Kallikaks' misfortune.[10]

Goddard's conclusion, that intelligence is as directly heritable as hair color or the shape of a nose, proved difficult to dislodge. By the time his book went out of print in 1939, the American public, as well as most scientific experts, were convinced that nature had destined some people to succeed and others to fail. "The answer is in a word 'Heredity,'" said Goddard. "Bad stock."[11]

We can see now why our turn-of-the-century Paris vacationers from the last chapter endured so much skepticism about their adopted son. By that time, heredity had been thoroughly enlisted in support of racial hierarchy and imperial conquest. Biology was destiny, determining that certain races would be eternal also-rans, while others—this was when words like *Aryan* and *Nordic* entered the popular vocabulary—would always be smarter and stronger. Public opinion was buttressed by reams of scientific-looking books and charts illustrating the connection between skull size and the advance of Western civilization. In a democratic society, everyone was theoretically equal—but that did not mean they all had to end up in the same place or be treated as if they might. Heredity offered important social explanations in an age of great wealth and dire poverty, imperial conquest and colonization.

It shouldn't surprise us that adoptees started appearing in a lot of studies. In the early 1920s, Margaret Cobb, a researcher at the Yale University Clinic of Child Development, surveyed two hundred "adoptable" children, relinquished by the parents and referred to her from the Connecticut Department of Child Welfare. She gathered as much background information as she could, including on the children's families of origin and their early upbringing, but based most of her conclusions on a new tool for measuring intelligence, the Stanford-Binet test. This tool allowed Cobb to rank each child by a number, their intelligence quotient or IQ.[12]

The news was not good: The adoptable children all lagged behind their peers. The reason, according to Cobb, was not their difficult life experiences but the fact that they were born feeble-minded. Like produced like. Only about 2 percent of her subjects, said Cobb, had any college potential; not many more, about 7 percent, were even likely to finish high school. This study, published by the eminent child psychologist Arnold Gesell in 1923, served as a warning about adoption, the potential for tragedy in "under-placing" dull children with bright parents, or "over-placing" smart children in homes unlikely to meet their intellectual needs.[13]

Thankfully, this was not the last word. Other nature-nurture studies, beginning in the 1930s, cast doubt on Cobb's dire predictions and her less-than-hopeful picture of adoptive parenting. A 2007 analysis of Korean adoptees, for example, found that their home environments mattered a lot, not so much whether children and parents were an intellectual match, but how parents modeled and shaped important life choices. The study tracked "social outcomes," whether adopted children aspired to competitive colleges, whether they married or drank alcohol. One of the key factors was family size: Adoptees with one other sibling were far more likely to stay in school and 16.1 percent more likely to graduate from college, compared to their peers in larger less-educated families. As the researcher hypothesized, "The quantity and quality of parental attention matters a tremendous amount for adoptees outcomes."[14]

Yet still, when we applied to an adoption agency in the 1980s, intelligence was a key question. And perhaps not surprisingly: I had finished a PhD, and my husband had his MDiv from seminary and was on his way to a doctorate in ministry. Our social workers understood, but did not state directly, that any placement would have to be fair to us—and probably even more so to whoever became our child. And so they chose Nate for us, who came from a clearly exceptional Vietnamese refugee family, one with lots of education and mechanical aptitude. To no one's surprise, Nathan can fix anything, and even better, loves doing so. But the funny part is that of all the children and grandchildren in my birth family, he is the most like my own father, a research physicist who also loved to fix things. My siblings are smart, and every one of them has a clear aptitude for science. Yet in all kinds of ways, Nate was my dad's soulmate. He is the only person on record who has actually repeatedly asked to help my dad in his basement workshop—we had all learned through hard experience that "helping" really meant watching, for a long, long time. He is the one my dad, in his final days, trusted with our family's most prized heirloom, a magnificent grandfather clock, the masterpiece of that basement workshop. Nate was, we all understood, the only one in the entire extended family who actually knew how it worked.

Anna's birth mother chose our file from among other prospective parents because we were both "doctors" and she was worried about her baby's health. She had no way of knowing from our paperwork that neither of those degrees had any practical, much less lifesaving, value.

But here's the final truth: In the end, none of the concerns about intelligence and education mattered. Both Nate and Anna were smart and self-aware, eager and curious and quick to learn—and they also hated going to school. Public education in the 1990s, when we lived in Cambridge, was extraordinarily vigilant about learning disabilities and attention deficit disorders, and like many adoptive parents who have weathered a complicated bureaucratic process, we were not shy about getting help. Both children had tutors and special reading classes, and, in spite of homework nightmares and morning meltdowns, did fine in grammar school. But neither of them finished college. Nate loved fixing cars more than any of the engineering courses he was taking; Anna was too full of energy to sit still in a classroom. Before long, she was traveling the country as a roadie for musicians with pit bulls and face tattoos—and, I hasten to add, some of the nicest people you will ever meet.

FAMILY TREES

For many years, I was executive director of a small, idiosyncratic archive situated at the top of Boston's Beacon Hill. "Quaint" does not even begin to describe its surroundings. That neighborhood includes some of the oldest and most famous real estate in the city, rows of redbrick townhouses and long shady streets with rambling redbrick sidewalks. The most famous Brahmin haunts, however, are right below the archive windows, resting peacefully in Boston's iconic Granary Burial Ground. My closest neighbors were legendary puritans and patriots, the likes of Samuel Sewall, Paul Revere, and Samuel Adams.

Not surprisingly, many of our living visitors were ardent genealogists, eager to extract proof of New England ancestry from our archives. A lot of them zeroed in on more famous figures: I got used to hearing from a would-be researcher, "I'm a descendant of John Winthrop," the first governor of the Massachusetts Bay Colony.

I wanted to answer (but never did), that I am too. After four centuries of human intermingling, so is pretty much any random soul walking down Beacon Street.

This claim of mine, I've since discovered, is pretty much right. Statisticians have poked numerous holes in our idea of genealogy as a single tree with forking branches. Carl Zimmer—who has written a book with a title I could not turn away from, *She Has Her Mother's Laugh: The Powers, Perversions, and Potential of Heredity*—explains that, if you go far back enough in time, the tree model of heredity "explodes into impossibility." It is a woefully simplistic understanding of how heredity actually works. When you consider the total reality, any path of descent from John Winthrop, much less Charlemagne or Genghis Khan, involves trillions of different forks and multitudes more individual people, a universe of begettings and begats. Statistically speaking, says Zimmer, every European alive today is a descendant of Charlemagne.[15]

Yet genealogy remains an enormously popular hobby—a fact even more curious, given its aristocratic origins. In the nineteenth century, we the people of the United States, the proud owners of the world's newest democracy, became obsessed with family trees. Until that time, keeping track of relatives was a problem for the elites, burdened as they were with ancestral estates and rising threats of revolution from the hoi polloi. It took a while for Americans to get past the obvious snob-appeal of genealogical research, but, as is generally true where money and novelty are involved, they managed. By the mid-nineteenth century, the United States had its own corps of gentleman genealogists and antiquarians ready and able to trace anyone's ancestry back to the Mayflower or Pocahontas, even William the Conqueror, provided you gave them the right amount of money and time. With the aid of a trained genealogist, an ordinary run-of-the-mill American might become a Knickerbocker or Puritan, a Huguenot or an Anglo-Saxon. Genealogy made cultural sense in a country with a complicated past and a wide variety of newcomers. Ancestral origins bestowed a bit of order, maybe even a sense of collective identity, a logic of belonging to something beyond oneself.

There was a more sinister aspect, however. Behind the zeal for genealogy was the idea of "blood," the word we use for a relationship that is proverbially thicker than water. Use of that term began as a way of sorting out animals—falcons and racehorses and greyhounds—but it could also be turned on people. In the history of Western society, "noble blood" was not biological, not an A-positive or B-negative trait but an ineffable something, the source of admirable moral traits like bravery or chivalry and even superior physical endowments. It should be no surprise that the idea of "blood relations" emerged about the same time that Europeans began encountering other people with different skin colors and hair textures, people who might be forcibly enlisted to build European empires overseas. Here was a way to put and keep people in their places, restricting kinship to a traceable family tree but also explaining why you are better than the rest and deserve to be treated accordingly.

In other words, blood is a thoroughly aristocratic concept with a nasty history, from racialized slavery to twentieth-century fascism. And yet it informs so much of how we think and talk about family identities, inherited traits—and about adoption—despite a shift in scientific understanding of how genes work, what they do and do not do.

NEW GENETICS

Generations of Kallikaks would be glad to know that the emerging understanding of nature and nurture is both balanced and subtle. As it turns out, we are much more than what's dictated by our DNA. Our environment matters, steering and molding our biological makeup in ways that are sometimes even measurable. You and I are who we are, at least partly, because of *epigenic* factors, which include our behaviors—for example, what we eat and how we exercise—and our surrounding culture. "A lone Neanderthal growing up playing video games and watching movies in its enclosure in the primate research institute," write the authors of the book *Extended Heredity*, "would surely fail to develop many of the behavior peculiarities of its species." Our "couch-potato Neanderthal" would look like his ancestors but also, the authors claim, like a "modern, industrialized *Homo sapiens*, with its proverbial joy-stick thumb, fondness for potato chips, and alarming body-mass index."[16]

It now appears that life events, both good and bad, can change the way DNA is expressed physically—and how it is passed down to the next generation. A study of Union army soldiers in Confederate prison camps, for example, found that the suffering these men endured not only shortened their own lives but those of their children born after the war ended. The sons of POWs had an 11 percent higher mortality rate than those of other veterans. Interestingly, their daughters did not, leading to the possibility of a sex-linked genetic trait on the Y chromosome. The mortality effect was also absent in children born before their fathers went to war. Other studies focusing on Holocaust survivors found the trauma resonating across generations, with measurable increases in cortisol, a hormone connected to stress responses.[17]

This research is controversial, and we are far from an equation determining the separate influences of nature and nurture—perhaps fortunately. Clearly, however, we are approaching much more expansive explanations for why and how we become who we are. Take the example of little monkeys with a short serotonin transponder allele—in other words, a genetic predisposition to impulsivity, aggression, and depression. When raised by "adequate" mothers, they have no serotonin deficit. The same appears to be true of humans: A history of childhood abuse will wreak havoc on someone with a genetic tendency for depression, but a safe and loving environment can leave such a tendency dormant. "Children who are fortunate enough to have an attuned and attentive parent," writes psychologist Bessel van der Kolk, "are not going to develop this genetically related problem."[18]

Some scientists, says Carl Zimmer, have begun to insist on a more expansive definition of heredity, one that takes into account all of the environmental input and mysterious bodily processes that create a unique individual. They have even taken a second look at the famous studies of identical twins separated at birth, which, back in the mid-twentieth century, found near perfect correlation on intelligence tests. Not only were some of the results of those studies deeply suspect—perhaps even the results of fraud—they were far too neat to be believable. Identical twins, according to more recent data, do score more alike on intelligence tests than fraternal twins, and even those raised apart from each other end up more similar than different. But scientists currently estimate heritability at roughly 50 percent—not a negligible figure but also not proof that smart always begets smart, no matter the circumstances.[19]

UNMOORED FROM BIOLOGY

When our children were little, the book of choice about adoption was *The Chosen Baby*, by Valentina P. Wasson. The title says it all. A woman who had loved the story as a child said it gave her the impression that "being adopted [was] like a superpower. I was part of an elite part of humanity. I was special." I remember reading it to Nate and Anna and getting swept up in that message: We were a family that was meant to be.

Now I have a few second thoughts about the book, as do plenty of childcare professionals. The protagonists, Mr. and Mrs. Brown, who have been thoroughly vetted by the Lady from a "Home," literally pick out the baby they want, after first turning down another perfectly good infant. "This is a beautiful child," they tell the Lady, "but we know it is not our baby." The next child is just as cute and lovely, and this time, when Mrs. Brown picks him up and puts him on her lap, he smiles at her. The couple agree instantly. "This is our Chosen Baby. We don't have to look any further."[20]

It shouldn't surprise anyone that the book was written in 1939, updated with new illustrations in the 1950s. The story comes from a time when couples did indeed go and pick out the child they wanted, and when every effort was being made to give adoption a warm, positive spin, especially to young children. By the 1980s, the choosing had been somewhat reversed—in our case, the birth parents chose us from among several other families. The underlying message of the book now seems unnerving: You could have been turned down as easily as you were selected. Baby Number One was every bit as adorable as Number Two—why did one get sent back to his crib and the other to a loving home?

In this context, the whole notion of choice itself seems problematic. In the story, Mr. and Mrs. Brown are fully in charge of a big life decision, as if we're all a set of problems to be managed and taken care of. I want to know what happened ten, twenty, thirty years after they took their baby home.

Like any parent, I wonder what I could have done better, where I should have pushed more or pulled a little harder. I also worry about the effect of generational trauma, the fact that both of my children had birth parents whose families were deeply scarred by the war in Southeast Asia. Or beyond that, the stress and sadness their birth mothers endured while Nathan and Anna were gestating. What, I wonder, could I or should I have done differently?

Then again, I am fairly certain that any biological child I may have had would not have called me late at night from under a bridge, reportedly "somewhere" between Germany and the Netherlands, having been abruptly fired by the dysfunctional family that had hired her as a nanny. I would not have figured out how to get her home from a visit to a goat farm in rural Arkansas in a matter of hours, where her birth mother was rapidly destabilizing. I would not have received a phone call from a storage container in Big Sur where she was living with her soon-to-be husband, a Hungarian short-order cook.

I would not have had to prepare myself for the death of my child in an emergency room, watching my son struggle to breathe as he fought anaphylactic shock from an allergy I had no way of anticipating.

My adopted children have even changed the look of my driveway. Right now, two improbable cars share a patch of blacktop with our plain and prudent Subaru Outback. They are also Subarus—we are brand loyal in our family—but they're built for racing, for aggressively blowing the doors off of anything else on the road. One of the cars is a gray WRX with a roll bar nearly as tall as the car roof and a hood intake that looks like a giant snarl, and the other is electric blue and low-slung, a BRZ with an engine so beefy that it sets all the windows in our house to rattling. I've seen how fast that blue car can go, holding my sense of doom in check while I watched my son tear around a professional-grade race track, streaking past and cornering with a terrifying squeal.

Growing up, I had most of my adventures reading books in my backyard treehouse. Of course, I dreamed of running away on a raft or hitchhiking to California, and once I earned a week of detention for skipping classes. I briefly smoked cigarettes. But, for the most part, life was uneventful; our home was stable and safe, with the usual run of childhood accidents and sibling conflicts. That would have been okay, but think of all I might have missed by not adopting these particular children. I owe every one of the aforementioned surprising, terrifying, intriguing, and personal-growth-enhancing experiences to them. Perhaps the lack of a biological relationship is a little bit freeing. "Being unmoored from the biological tie is a relief," says adoptive father Nicholas Christakis. "I don't see a reflection of my (neurotic) self in my boy, and no one asks him to shoulder that burden either, though he recently did complain that he worried my nerdiness was 'wearing off' on him."[21]

In the next chapter, we will look more closely at the image and reality of a "good mother." In the meantime, I can only appeal to some hard-won knowledge. I have had to learn, sometimes the hard way, that there are lots of ways to live a successful life, more reasons to worry yourself sick and to laugh yourself into exhaustion than anyone could imagine.

CHAPTER 5

MOTHERS AND OTHERS

At some point, I stopped making jokes about my mothering skills. When I said that I prepared for a night out by spreading newspapers on the floor and leaving the kids an extra water dish, did I notice—or did I imagine—a moment of hesitation? Did they think I was serious? When I told people that I had run out of orange juice and given Anna and Nathan orange soda for breakfast, I thought I saw them staring at me for a millisecond, seemingly deciding whether the story was true. Everyone laughed when Erma Bombeck or Rosanne Barr made fun of their kids, because they knew that, after all the snide belittling, both of those women went home, paid the babysitters, and served their children fresh-squeezed orange juice. Perhaps in my case, they weren't so sure. Maybe because I had not given birth or lactated, there was no guarantee that I would be a good mother. For all they knew, I might lack some essential instinct of care, an extra something, an ability that blinked on after a woman gave birth.

This chapter is about the terrifically complicated dynamics of modern motherhood, but not just for women of a certain age and status. Same-sex couples, families with two dads or one dad, or grandparents who are raising children—or even those who are childless—are also part of this story. It turns out that there are lots of ways for a lot of different people to be moms.

Before we get there though, we have to sift through a lot of cultural assumptions about motherhood. Historian Julie Berebitsky writes about the "unspoken hierarchy" that places the experience of childbirth at the very top, as the truest entryway to parenthood. The true test, she says, is "biology, not nurturance."[1] In that sense, adoption feels very different, almost like membership without the necessity of paying dues. "By adopting, I was not a full-fledged mother," one woman writes. Not having "paid the price of pregnancy" or won "the badge of labor or the award for delivery," she would be forever an outsider, "an associate member at best. I looked like the other women, but I felt like less of one."[2]

After all, motherhood is supposed to be natural. In how many books and movies does pregnancy transform selfish women into earth mothers? How many ways are we told that childless women are brittle and self-absorbed, perhaps not even truly female? We don't question the premise of *The Handmaid's Tale*, for instance, which pits young and fertile women against the old and sterile, who are selfishly allied with selfish men. Critics went through the roof when the (fictional) television character Murphy Brown had a baby out of wedlock. But no one seemed to mind what was to me the more appalling moment, when she sang the Carole King anthem "(You Make Me Feel Like) A Natural Woman" to her baby.

Anyone who has been a mother—or everyone who has had one—knows that maternal love is a terrifically complicated emotion. When the baby wakes up and cries every two hours until morning or the teenager deliberately turns off her cell phone so you can't reach her, affection can turn to rage without warning. When a little being pours cereal on your lap or lets the cat outside, the natural response is not a beatific smile. Even on a good day, the relentless responsibility is wearying, the mundane round of duties irritating, even thankless. We love our children deeply and desperately, but that's not the end of the story.

I entered motherhood with some complicated feelings: an unstable mix of guilt and gratitude and a determination to do the right thing at every turn. I was, after all, a stand-in for two deprived teenage birth mothers, the recipient of their gifts beyond measure. In all the years since, I have never forgotten that reality. I have been a mother just like other mothers, wiping noses and changing diapers, but in other ways, I am not like other mothers at all. I am not quite real.

A STORY ABOUT MOTHERHOOD

Once upon a time, motherhood was not a psychological high-wire act. Women gave birth and took care of children, but they did a lot of other things too. They made meals, washed and mended clothes, cleaned the house and tended gardens. All these necessary tasks in the days before running water and shopping malls could take hours, sometimes days to finish. There was relatively less time to nurture a little one's personality or hone their intellectual skills. Or even, unfortunately, to keep a close eye on them. Historian Laurel Thatcher Ulrich tells the tragic eighteenth-century story of the Newell family, whose little one wandered off their property and drowned in a shallow pit of water. When Thomas Newell sued his neighbor for negligence, Mrs. Newell testified in court that she had only let the boy out of her sight for an hour or maybe even just half an hour. ("Eek!" says everyone who has ever watched a toddler for more than five minutes.) Alice Walton's son also drowned in an unfenced water hole while she was out in the fields bringing her husband dinner. The older sister who was supposed to be watching the ill-fated toddler said, "[He] was just here. Just now presently."[3]

These are stories of unspeakable heartbreak, painful to read even centuries later. We almost want to believe that the constant risk of childhood death caused parents to love their children less. In fact, historians once supposed that the old practice of passing down a name from a dead sibling to a new baby signaled emotional detachment, a matter-of-fact acceptance of loss. But the truth is that, for some basic practical reasons, a three-year-old might end up on his own for hours at a time, exploring shallow pits of water. Children simply could not be watched at every moment. Their mothers had work to do. Old-fashioned motherhood, as Ulrich says, was "extensive" rather than "intensive."[4]

The dangers did not end with the colonial period. In the 1890s, for example, children under five accounted for about 40 percent of all deaths. Two out of ten would die before their tenth birthday. Before the widespread availability of vaccines, diseases like measles and diphtheria were a constant ominous presence. Children also faced regular dangers from city streets—dying as a result of accidents involving carriages and trolleys, then cars and trucks. In contrast, today, according to *The New England Journal of Medicine,* the instance of childhood deaths is 2 percent of the total number of fatalities, a number which includes not just very young children but adolescents as well.[5]

There is a healthy dose of modern privilege behind the belief that child-rearing is a mother's primary job, easily more important than any other domestic duties. The best moms do not have spotless houses, we are reminded; they forget the laundry and the breakfast dishes and sit down on the floor to play Candyland with the children. We forget that for most women throughout most of human history, there was no such choice. The family could have food on the table and decent clothes to wear, or they could go without. The same would be true for many women around the world today. Hardworking mothers in Somalia and Guatemala and Laos certainly love their children, but they do not have the luxury of sitting down to read the cultural equivalent of *The Very Hungry Caterpillar* with a toddler in the middle of the day.

With modern privilege came new liabilities. The Victorian era gave us an exalted view of motherhood, a sentimental conviction that maternal love was the pinnacle of all human affections. At once a biological imperative and spiritual gift, a natural instinct and divinely ordained role, becoming a mother was the fundamental destiny of every woman. Behind all the poetry and flowers, however, there was a growing suspicion, a worry that instinct was not enough. Modern life was getting complicated, with all kinds of new choices and decisions. Perhaps the average mother was just not up to the job.

By the early twentieth century, child-rearing manuals were a must for every responsible parent, a staple of the family bookshelf with expert advice available every step of the way, from diapers to high school diplomas. These how-to books argued that all those beloved home remedies and crude punishments—centuries of lore about chicken soup and father's belt, handed down from mothers and grandmothers—were actually bad for children. No more old wives' tales, no more reliance on maternal instinct alone. Wise parents heeded the advice of experts, from Arnold Gesell to Dr. Spock, the only way to ensure they were doing the best job possible. Never mind that the experts tended to reverse their advice every few decades, based on the latest scientific evidence.

In a way, this new version of the nature-nurture equation gave the adoptive mother a built-in advantage. What they might have lacked in maternal instinct they gained in outside certification. True, they had entered motherhood via an unnatural route, bypassing pregnancy and childbirth and heading straight into diapers and formula. But, unlike the average mother, they had been screened by professionals; experts had declared them fit to parent a child. Even better, adoptive parents were not saddled with the random result of a careless sexual act. They were parents on purpose and matched with the perfect child. If anything, up through the late twentieth century, the American adoption system confirmed the prevailing ideology about motherhood, and then did it one better.

This image of the perfect adoptive mother was deeply conservative—a primary reason why, until recently, single women were all but completely sidelined by adoption agencies. What was once considered acceptable—an eccentric Miss Havisham or a well-heeled movie star like Joan Crawford adopting a child—was by the post–World War II era starting to look unnatural. Not getting married was reason enough for suspicion, and deciding to parent a child without a father was beyond the pale.

The road to approved motherhood was narrow, even for the more upstanding sorts. Too much talk about adoptive parents and children as "chosen" people and you ended up with the reverse, the troubling possibility that what was chosen could, at least theoretically, be unchosen. Perhaps because adoptive parents had become mothers and fathers on purpose, their love was conditional. Perhaps because it was a deliberate decision, it was not spiritually pure. This is why my jokes about motherhood were not always received as funny, why I was instinctively careful not to complain about dirty diapers or a stalled professional career. Someone might take me too seriously. I might, after all, not be a good mother.

BONDING AND SCIENCE

One of the best-known books about adoption, David Kirk's *Shared Fate*, published in 1964, held scant hope for normal family life. Unlike natural parents, who grew up with plenty of role models to follow, adoptive parents had none. They were left adrift, without a "cultural script." In a word, said Kirk, they were "normless."[6] Not only were they handicapped from the start by the psychological wound of infertility, they had to figure out how to raise their children while walking through unmapped territory, ridden with moral minefields. On the one hand, adoptive parents could choose to live a lie, to act as if they were "real," as if their love was as deep and authentic as that of a biological mother or father. Or they could tell their children the truth, that they were essentially playacting, pretending to be a "real" family. Either way was a betrayal of trust, and either way, the likely result was injury, if not outright failure. How could adoptive parents not become insecure and overprotective, overcompensating with their troubled, clingy children?

The science was not helping. By the middle of the twentieth century, after the world had weathered two wars that upended the lives of millions of children, researchers discovered a disturbing legacy. The evidence was becoming painfully clear that any disruption of the mother-infant bond, any deprivation of the child's fundamental need for maternal love and care risked deep and lasting psychological trauma.

How do adoptive parents—more specifically adoptive mothers—bond with their children? Nathan's first month with us was exhausting and wild, but also very simple. One night, when he was enjoying yet another bottle that, technically at least, he did not need—I was on high alert those early days—he paused and looked at me. I already loved him deeply, even fiercely, but I wondered if he felt the same. Did he know I was his mother? Or was I just someone feeding him a bottle of formula at two a.m.? I will never forget how, in one amazing moment, a shiver passed through my entire body, a physical sensation of love and connection. I had to believe he somehow felt it too, caught something radiating from the center of my soul. Was it a shot of oxytocin, the proverbial "love hormone"? Or something more mystical, more spiritual? Nate kept on with his bottle, nonchalant as ever, but I believed, and still believe, that something important happened in those moments. I became more than his caregiver—I was really and truly his mother.

Anna's homecoming, however, was all you might expect if you dropped a three-month-old infant into a pastor's family four days before Christmas. Three-year-old Nathan was not ready for competition and found many different ways to demonstrate his displeasure—parading past with the dog's overflowing water dish while I was trapped on the couch feeding the baby, squirting the Christmas Eve Communion grape juice onto his father's white preaching robe moments before the service. It did not help that our new baby did not appear to like us very much. When she was not fussing over everything, she appeared to ignore us, sleeping for hours on end. I know now that this is her way of managing stress; Anna is and has always been an expert sleeper. But in those first few days, what would have been a blessing to any other mother of a three-month-old, I took as a sign of rejection.

Nor did it help that I was a mother in the 1980s, when popular opinion on child-rearing was all about the absolute primacy of the mother-child bond. Breastfeeding moms were popping up everywhere, in shopping malls and train stations and church pews, serenely defiant and bared in public. In fact, shortly after meeting Nathan, I read and briefly considered one adoptive mother's account of successful lactation. Thank God, I decided that the reward was not worth the manual labor involved.

That popular opinion was no passing phase, however. It drew on decades of scientific opinion, much of it going back to the 1940s and psychologist René Spitz's short but haunting documentary *Grief*. Spitz's film depicted, in grainy black and white, the stark suffering endured by abandoned infants. The visual evidence was shocking, even bizarre, babies wagging their heads and rocking in their cribs, unable even to cry beyond a "thin wail." Even a temporary separation of a few weeks or months was psychologically devastating to a baby, said Spitz, as disorienting and damaging as if a child had been suddenly "dumped on another continent in an alien environment where nobody speaks its language[,] and customs and food are foreign." Far too many of them, Spitz warned his viewers, would end up "mentally impaired, antisocial, criminal, or insane."[7]

The psychologist John Bowlby gave the problem a name. The Second World War, he said, had spawned an epidemic of *attachment disorder*. In the 1950s, he was recruited by the World Health Organization to report on the children made homeless by the devastation. He published this work in a widely-read book, *Child Care and the Growth of Love*. Bowlby's research pointed to a ringing and urgent conclusion, that all children needed consistent loving relationships, not just to thrive but to survive. "Prolonged deprivation" of a mother's care, he warned, would have "grave and far-reaching effects" on the child's character and "the whole of his future life."[8] Bowlby's work was particularly groundbreaking in the attention it gave to the emotional needs of newborns and infants. He treated them as individuals with unique thought processes and inner lives. A baby was not just a blank slate, a messy mix of Freudian drives and desires, but an exquisitely complex being who required—deserved—the nurture and protection of wise and loving adults.

THE PROBLEM WITH ATTACHMENT THEORY

The question is obvious: What about adopted children? Did their early experiences of leaving their birth mothers mean they were destined for a life of separation anxiety? The studies started coming out in the 1960s, led by Marshall Schechter, a psychiatrist treating patients in Beverly Hills, California. Analyzing his own records of troubled children, he announced an alarming trend: Adoptees were one hundred times more likely to suffer serious emotional problems than the average child. The reason, according to Schechter, was adoption itself, a permanent "narcissistic injury" caused by the primary rejection by the child's birth parent, a wound destined to haunt every adopted child for their entire lifetime. Other studies, building on attachment theory, corroborated Schechter's findings, warning of disordered attachments, a "primary affect hunger" that could only result in a lifetime of psychological pain.[9]

The argument was controversial then, as it is now. It turned out, first of all, that Schechter was basing his conclusions on a tiny sample—his famously troubled adoptees amounted to only sixteen cases out of the 120 he had examined. Moreover, some of his evidence was purely anecdotal:

A colleague, Povl Toussieng, a researcher at the Menninger Clinic, had apparently mentioned that a third of the children under treatment were adopted, a statement widely accepted though never verified through the usual academic channels of peer review and collegial critique. Despite the wobbly foundation, however, disordered attachments and emotional trauma continue to be a standard part of the professional literature on adoption and public perception. (We will pick up the discussion of bonding and attachment again in the next chapter.)

The strongest criticisms of attachment theory come from anthropologists and evolutionary biologists, people who study non-Western cultures. They are not at all surprised at how closely this theory tracks one particular ideal, our modern nuclear family with two parents providing exclusive and ongoing care for their children, from infancy to adulthood. But is that the only healthy possibility? Attachment theory assumes that the goal of every parent is a well-adjusted, independent adult, a "self-sufficient, self-contained, and separate self," as anthropologist Heidi Keller puts it. Yet, she writes, that particular set of assumptions applies "only to a small part of the world's population."[10]

The Efe hunter-gatherers in the Congo, for example, do not have the modern luxury of round-the-clock care in a household that is separate and independent from other families. The members of this group must cooperate in order to survive. Efe children are raised by a network of neighbors and kin, sometimes a surprisingly large one. Researchers found that in any given two-hour period, the average infant would be cared for by an average of nine caregivers or "social partners." If we put stock in attachment theory, we would worry about the loss of a primary maternal bond and wonder whether all that handing off of children from one neighbor to another was going to inflict long-term psychological pain. But in fact, those children do extremely well. Even more, it looks like interacting with many different adults with diverse caregiving styles and an array of personalities makes Efe children more tolerant and flexible. In academic speak, it provides them with a "complex set of behaviors for developing, sustaining, and renewing relationships." In layperson's terms, this translates to happy children with an expansive sense of trust, as well as a particular neurobiological ability to "manage attention" and regulate their emotions.[11]

While the hunter-gatherer lifestyle is not for everyone, of course, there's no denying that inner strength and independence are valuable, even necessary traits for anyone looking to succeed in the modern world today. But that doesn't rule out that there are other kinds of spiritual and psychological well-being. We must always remember that what we in the West enshrine as normal—that is, best—is actually rare within the flow of human experience.

Other researchers argue that our brains are far more flexible and nimble than we give them credit for. Perhaps a difficult experience early in life is not a psychological dead end. Perhaps most lives offer more opportunity for healing and transformation than we think.[12]

MATERNAL INSTINCT?

Take for example our understanding of that old yet strangely durable sacred cow: the concept of the maternal instinct. For so long, we have assumed that the act of giving birth changes everything. Whether through a hormonal change or by the will of an all-knowing, all-powerful God, we'd like to believe that the result is the same: A latent sacrificial urge is released, and an ordinary run-of-the-mill woman becomes extraordinary, equipped by nature to care for her children, even to defend them to the death. For proof, we're told, just look at the animal kingdom. Ask anyone who has run afoul of a mother bear with cubs or watched a bird mom tirelessly stuffing worms into the beaks of her ravenous offspring. The internet even gives us glimpses of adorably altruistic dogs and cats nursing each other's orphaned kittens and pups. Our entire class of animals, after all, takes its name from something only biological mothers can do, nurse their offspring with those famously lactating mammalian glands, which have been worshipped, fetishized, mocked, and embraced in human culture over the course of centuries. What could be more natural, more instinctive than motherhood?

The problem is that an awful lot of animals are terrible mothers. Some, in fact, literally eat their young; Dracula ants suck the blood of their offspring. Then there's the quokka, a small Australian marsupial. Faced with attacking dingoes, she opens her pouch, drops her babies, and runs away—after which she breezes off to have another litter.[13]

Here's the thing: The science strongly suggests that motherhood is not an automatic hormonal response awakened by pregnancy and childbirth. It is a learned behavior. Mother love clicks in after the baby arrives, activated by the actual physical process of caring for an infant. Take the example of what evolutionary anthropologist Sarah Hrdy calls the "au pair from hell." A "virgin" female rat, meaning one that has never been a mother or spent any time around baby rats, is about as non-maternal as you can get. In other words, she will either eat or ignore any baby rat she comes across. Yet there is hope for our nightmare babysitter. Once she is repeatedly exposed to rat pups, she will begin to nurture rather than kill them. If baby rats are placed in her cage enough times, she will mother them effectively and devotedly—and here's the point: All of this happens without having undergone any of the hormonal change associated with pregnancy.[14]

Human beings are similar. It's the act of caring for infants that makes us maternal, not the other way around. In fact, the experience of nurturing actually remaps our brains. It gives us a particular kind of attentiveness, the ability to "read" an infant's signals and attend to them. Everyone who has ever cared for a baby knows how hard this is. I find it comforting to know that our brains can help us to figure out whether that's a tired cry, a hungry one, or just a baby who's bored and needs attention. A study of forty-seven first-time mothers tracked these physical changes over time. As new moms cared for their infants, they developed new neurological capabilities—technically, this means a stronger connection from the right and left amygdala to other key regions in the brain. That connectivity made them better at "maternal structuring." Their brains were learning how to pay the right amount of attention to an infant and then to respond the best way—with a clean diaper, some food, or just a cuddle.[15]

These neurological changes are possible, says Hrdy, because we are primates. Just like apes and chimpanzees, we love babies. Our disproportionately large heads mean that we cannot gestate as long as we might like, and so our children are born unable to do pretty much anything. Because they are weak and small, incapable of getting up and running off, human and primate moms can be sure that a baby is hers. The chances of mistakenly caring for someone else's infant are slim. We have the luxury of coddling.[16]

That's not true for all animals, even all mammals. Female sheep, for example, will abandon a newborn unless they form a bond with it immediately after birth. Her little lamb is, after all, capable of getting up and running off from a predator hours after it is born. A new mother must imprint her smell on the baby by licking it, or the game is up. Without that sensory connection, says Hrdy, the "door to maternal tolerance slams shut."[17]

Humans and primates love babies—and not just their own but babies in general. We are biologically attuned to hold them, play with them, and keep them close, whether or not there is a genetic connection. Not all of us do, of course, but we are still absolutely capable of caring for other mothers' children. We are, according to Hrdy, capable of being good adoptive parents, perhaps especially female partners in a same-sex relationship. "Children can be adopted days after birth and loved just as intensely, as ferociously," she writes, "as those babies whose bodies passed through their mother's birth canal and then pressed against her right after birth." Primatologists were not surprised, for example, when Binta Jua, a gorilla at Chicago's Brookfield Zoo, cuddled the little boy who had fallen into her enclosure. When a primate mother takes in an orphaned baby or finds a substitute for one she has lost, the process is seamless. Relationships between mothers and adopted infants, says Hrdy, are "indistinguishable from those of mothers and offspring they gave birth to." It's the experience of "physical proximity over time," not a particular scent or a genetic bond, that creates primate mothers.[18]

Here's the other important thing: We are learning that it's not just women who change with the presence of infants, who become attentive mothers—it's *people*. In other words, the neurological remapping researchers found in new mothers also happens in new fathers, which means that it is available to same-sex couples, including those with two dads. What's more, studies found that men who took care of babies changed, not just as caregivers but as human beings. They became better at processing their own emotions and responding to those of others. When a man or a woman becomes a parent, says journalist Chelsea Conaboy, the self "extends a little further." It learns to encompass another. "All human adults have the capacity to develop as caregivers," she tells us. "All human adults, not only birth parents, are fundamentally changed by the act of parenting."[19]

The new findings on motherhood are not just good news for human adoptive parents, they are good news for everybody. We now know, says Conaboy, "that every person possesses the capacity to develop a parental caregiving network. We know enough to say that babies change the adults who care for them. We know enough to say that it is love and attention that ultimately shapes and creates the adapted parental brain, not exclusively a person's gender, sex, or method of procreation."[20] Mother love is a learned behavior that is theoretically available to all. The important part is the commitment, a decision made day after day, to care for a child.

After all, the essence of love is attentiveness. It's a matter not of the heart or the womb but of the eyes. It is about waiting and watching, attending to another, gaining a tolerance for empty time, learning the difficult discipline of patience. So much of parenthood is tending to someone else's needs for weeks and years and decades; so much of it is thoroughly, even mind-numbingly ordinary. It is looking up at the clock and realizing it is only 2:30, wondering how you will ever get to dinner and bedtime. It is lying in bed without sleeping, listening for the sound of a car in the driveway, of keys jingling and the back door opening, of a loved one now safe at home.

The philosopher Simone Weil describes attentiveness as a kind of self-emptying. It is a "negative effort," she says, the act of not doing rather than doing something. Giving attention is much more than concentrated looking, she says. It doesn't happen if you furrow your brow or nod at regular intervals—what you might expect in a therapist's office or a graduate school seminar. Those are surface performances, says Weil, and we often do them because we believe we'll be rewarded, maybe with reciprocal nods and smiles.[21] The right set of cues, the "uh huh" given at proper intervals might prompt the other person to carry out the same performance for me. True attention goes much deeper. It requires the "canceling of our desires," as philosopher and Weil biographer Robert Zaretsky explains. It happens when we allow the reality of another person to eclipse our own, when we turn away "from our blinding and bulimic self."[22]

Weil lived what she believed. She was a deeply reflective person, a mystic in fact, who lived a purposeful, strenuous life. Raised Jewish, she converted to Catholicism as an adult and served in the French Resistance during World War II. Weil was also a dedicated teacher but not the kind you would expect. Right answers, lectures, even grades, were profoundly unimportant to her. One of her students recalled how she would take her geometry class outside to sit under a tall cedar tree and "seek problems." "Reflecting on a problem," says Zaretsky, "rather than resolving it, was Weil's goal." Her students were to learn patience, because true discovery came not through relentless seeking but by waiting for insight. Even writing itself was an exercise in reflection, holding off on action until the right word would "come of itself at the end of our pen."[23]

Of course, complete, utter attentiveness, the kind that Weil describes, is completely impossible. For nineteenth-century feminist writer Margaret Fuller, the problem was "mountainous me," the restless ego that sneaks in at every opportunity, refusing to be sidelined.[24] Yet anyone who has ever cared for a child, not just for a stray afternoon but over the course of decades, receives an inkling of this truth, what it is like to empty, or at least delay, the self for the sake of another.

My life since graduate school has been a clinic in waiting—for a pregnancy, for a child, and for answers. Somehow, I used to think, there must be a good reason, a justification for the way life ended up. Perhaps there are lessons to be learned, grudges to be released. Maybe. The most satisfying explanation, to me anyway, comes from a character from one of my favorite novels, Robertson Davies's *Fifth Business*. He calls himself a "collaborator with Destiny"—I love that phrase—and not one "who put a pistol to its head and demanded particular treasures." The book takes its title from a (possibly made-up) theatrical term. A fifth business is an actor who is quietly essential to the plot but decidedly not the star of the show, that is, not in the role we tend to assume we were born to play. "We all think about ourselves as stars," he says, "and rarely recognize it when we are indeed mere supporting characters or even supernumeraries."[25] Life, in other words, is not a show in which I am the star—it is all about collaboration, with other people and with the circumstances which surround us all.

To me, it all comes down to surprises, whether or not I am open to the altogether unexpected, good or bad, pleasant or unpleasant. To me, that's not unlike raising a child who arrives as a near total enigma, a bundle of yet mysterious talents and abilities, loves and dislikes, needs and desires. That takes a particular kind of attentiveness, removing yourself from the foreground for the sake of another.

I wonder, though, what I might have already missed. I worry about blind spots. Would I have been tougher on a biological child—or more accommodating? Did the fact of our unrelatedness provide some distance, even a bit more objectivity, with my adopted children? That, I've decided, is a question worth another chapter.

CHAPTER 6

SEPARATING

"Hold on." The friend of a friend of a friend looked at me quizzically. "So both of your children are living at home?"

I winced at her emphasis on *both*.

I had a thousand explanations, practical and otherwise. Lots of millennials were temporarily back in the nest these days, right? And who wouldn't return to their childhood home with the indefensibly high cost of housing in the Boston area? True, it wasn't just the kids; it was the grandchildren and son-in-law too. Sure, that was a lot to contend with, but it was also temporary, and, anyway, was it so terrible? After all, we had a house and a yard, so why not give those beloved grandchildren some extra love from their extended family? Plus, we were saving the earth by sharing heat, water, and electricity.

It was hard not to feel defensive. So I nodded and said, "Yes." Then I added, "It's fabulous." With the emphasis on *fabulous*.

There's so much more to our story. One child swung back home on a short-term basis for some stability; the other was an indispensable housemate with all the practical skills my husband and I lacked, a person who knew what to do about the "check engine" light in the car or a mysterious beeping coming from somewhere down in the basement. On paper it all made perfect sense.

That's not to say I haven't wondered, more than once, whether the coming and going and staying was an adoption issue. Were my children, who at an early age had left one set of arms for another, trapped in some eternal loop of separation anxiety? Was something preventing them from making a clean break, a permanent flight from the nest?

I take comfort from a friend whose adopted son has circled in and out of the parental nest for most of his adult life. "They only leave when they are mad," he told me. And then, he said, eventually, they circle back. That might not be true for everyone, but I understand what he means. There's a particular kind of stickiness to adoptive relationships.

I still have questions though. In the late 1990s, when Nathan and Anna were just shy of middle school, we left Boston and moved to a small Midwestern city, where I had been offered a tenure-track position in a medium-sized liberal arts college. The decision had been agonizing for a whole list of reasons, some personal, some professional, and all of them familial. There were just so many unknowns, so many potential losses, so many risks. Would my husband find a job he liked? How would we survive in a place that was in many ways the reverse image of lefty liberal Cambridge? I worried about how white this Midwestern city was going to be, how conservative. And I worried how Nathan and Anna would handle the loss of friends and their old familiar city neighborhood.

For several years we had been part of a family study at the Harvard School of Public Health and had been paired with a psychologist, a kind and generous woman we had all come to trust. She knew our vulnerabilities but also urged us to go. We were more than capable, she said, of managing the transition.

I am still not sure whether she was right. Six years later, we were back in Boston, battered and limping and searching for therapists. We have stayed there ever since. It's home. I am left wondering if we made a bad decision, whether I had inflicted permanent and unnecessary damage on two people already dealing with a deep, unhealed wound.

Like so many other life moments, big transitions can feel different for adoptive families. That's not to say these aren't fraught for everyone else, especially when the basic financial costs of leaving home can be so forbidding. It's just that we take less for granted. I see it in the way writer Nicole Chung describes her relationship with her adoptive parents, how she felt when they assured her that she was somehow meant to be theirs, that she was their chosen child. "I've never doubted their love," she writes, "but sometimes I have wondered if my adoption added just a little more anxious weight to our disagreements and disparities, made us all feel a little less secure, in some hard and unspeakable way." Even with the sure faith that their differences would be resolved, an unspoken question remained:

> When what ties you to one another is not blood or birth or even mutual choice, but a piece of paper and a proclamation that you are family—when you haven't always belonged to one another, and can imagine countless scenarios in which you have remained strangers, never to meet, *is* there more vulnerability, perhaps more to fear, when some emotional or physical distance opens up between you?[1]

Even the prospect of outliving your parents falls differently when your connection began with their signatures on a set of legal documents. Beyond the pain of grieving a second separation, there is the unsettledness of it all. When one party dies, does the contract still exist? Can one end up, as Chung writes, "unadopted"?[2]

"I am now in my sixties," writes Mary Cardaras, "and my identity has become even more important, especially since the death of my adoptive parents. Without them I was left (again) untethered and wondering, *Who am I?*"[3]

I hear her. I have wondered, lived through, and watched others live through some of these same questions. When my adopted child was being absolutely incorrigible, pitching a tantrum for no good reason, I was not sure how angry I could get. Was she just being a normal strong-willed seven-year-old, or, in some unspoken way, was she testing me, seeing if I would give up and abandon her? How do you answer a question that no one dares to ask? I came to understand that the only way out of the emotional minefield was to sit her down and insist, calmly and clearly—and more than once—that there was nothing she could do to stop me from loving her.

Most of all, I wonder if we can ask our questions with a bit of grace. Might we take the pain of adoption seriously without cutting off all avenues of escape, without immediately going to pathology? There's no need to believe in easy stories of redemption, to insist that adoptive families are just incredibly lucky people who were somehow saved when they came together. Our relationships are complicated. Still, we don't need to assume that adoptive families are forever a step behind everyone else, that biological kinship is the only sure and safe alternative. Not everyone gets to live that way.

THE SEARCH MOVEMENT

It's hard to argue with a baby. Yet much of our contemporary conversation about the psychology of adoption has revolved around the most voiceless of all human beings, infants who are separated from their birth mothers and placed in adoptive homes. The psychologist Nancy Verrier was the first to suggest the idea of a "primal wound," in a book she published in 1993. Verrier warned that separating babies and birth mothers will always inflict psychological injury and worse, that the damage will be permanent, a sense of abandonment that never heals. In other words, according to Verrier, adoption is a lifelong post-traumatic situation, "a perpetual feeling of being a victim, of being powerless, of being helpless to help oneself."[4]

That linking of adoption with psychological trauma has fundamentally shaped our thinking. This is especially true when a child is going to be raised outside their native culture. An international adoption is an "epistemic injustice," as one academic researcher put it. Keeping a child in ignorance of their original culture, with its traditions and rituals, brings deliberate "harm to a person as a knower."[5] But any experience of separation, cross-cultural or not, is a problem. As another researcher warned, adoptees suffer a "trauma of consciousness," a memory of loss so deep that it is actually physical, imprinted on the body and ready to surface at a moment of crisis.[6]

Without a doubt, these feelings are real. "Any time I go through transition," interracial adoptee Rhonda Roorda writes, "the little girl in me cries out, 'Am I going to be okay?' It comes from the feeling of knowing," she says, "... that adults made decisions on my behalf as a child without necessarily considering the effect those decisions would have on me or even asking me what I thought, how I felt, and how those actions would change my trajectory lifelong."[7]

These worries are also more than theories, more than just some stray academic notion batted about in a genteel professional setting. In the 1970s and 1980s, warnings about primal loss and trauma fueled a vigorous social movement, one that challenged the entire practice and theory of adoption in the United States. Like so many of the causes of that era, this one invoked the language of individual rights, the insistence that every adoptee, just like every human being, deserved to know the story of their origins. In other words, adoption was no longer a private matter, an alternative way to build a family. It was, like racism and sexism and economic inequality, an injustice that demanded immediate restitution.

There were plenty of reasons for outrage: By the 1970s, laws governing adoption records had become painfully restrictive and unfair. We think of open adoptions as a recent change, but, in fact, for much of the twentieth century, records were not kept secret. State laws aimed primarily to preserve the reputations of birth parents, or as the state of Wisconsin put it, to keep "curious and unscrupulous persons" from obtaining information that might be used for blackmail.[8] Aside from that, anyone else with "good cause" could access birth or adoption records, and, in practice, that category was interpreted broadly. The basic principle was respect for privacy. In an age when out-of-wedlock pregnancies ruined lives and reputations, and possibly even set the stage for extortion, confidentiality was valuable and necessary.

Searches for birth parents were relatively rare and not necessarily fraught. Jean Paton, the first adoptee to speak publicly against closed records and secrecy, found her birth mother by looking her up at the Detroit courthouse. This was in the late 1940s, when adoptions were not nearly as controversial as they would later become. Paton pushed for a relatively low-key simple solution, a mutual-consent registry that would allow adoptees and birth parents to find each other if they so wished. At the time, it seemed like a good common-sense reform.

The biggest problems concerned the records themselves. Today we assume that everyone has something official to mark their birth, a certificate issued by the proper authorities and stored away in a government office. But that's a fairly recent custom. Less than a century ago, people did not generally march down to a state office building to verify that a baby had been born in the upstairs bedroom. They kept track in family Bibles or in church baptismal records. And why not? A lot of the time, it didn't particularly matter how old a person was. It took the era of big government, all of the changes that took place during and after World War II, to standardize recordkeeping. When millions of men and women joined the military or when their parents applied for Social Security retirement benefits, they all had to produce legal proof of age.

Then, just when recordkeeping became more systematic, adoptions became more private. A lot of that had to do with changing social attitudes toward untimely pregnancies. These were never desirable, of course, but a hundred or more years ago, when people lived in close-knit communities, where everybody knew or suspected who the father was, there were ways to hold people responsible. An out-of-wedlock baby was a public problem, not just a private sin. Adoptions were not always big secrets either. Birth mothers might be older women, perhaps even married or divorced and just unable to care for one more child. Adoptees were not necessarily infants either; they could be older children who had lost their parents or whose home situation simply fell apart. In these cases, privacy was important but not always possible, or, if the child was old enough to remember, even necessary.

After World War II, the ground rules changed. With all the GIs returning home, out-of-wedlock pregnancies soared. The typical birth mother was young, white, and middle-class: the suburban girl who "got in trouble." As we have seen, society wasted little sympathy on these girls. The social science of the day condemned her as damaged goods, neurotic and needy, and a poor reflection on her family. There were ways to keep the pregnancy secret, via the maternity home in the next county or a "vacation" with a supportive aunt. Moreover, given that most adoptees in the postwar era were infants, concealing the truth was both necessary and possible. One by one, state laws changed, and by the 1970s, sealed records were standard practice.

Then came the reckoning, when all those infants adopted under the veil of discretion became adults—and discovered that they were legally prohibited from seeing their own birth certificates. Florence Fisher was a fiercely articulate New York City housewife who found out about her adoption accidentally, while rummaging through a dresser drawer. She spent the next twenty years tracking down her birth mother. She told her story in a page-turning book, *The Search for Anna Fisher*, published in 1973. Although she was eventually able to find both of her birth parents, and took her birth father's last name, Fisher's fight to discover her identity was far from over. She did not see her original birth certificate until decades later, when, in 2020, the state of New York finally changed its secrecy laws. In the meantime, she started a movement. A brief notice in *The New York Times*, asking for other adoptees to contact her, brought an overwhelming response. Within a few years, she had founded the Adoptees Liberty Movement Association (ALMA), and it had grown to some fifty chapters and fifty thousand members. "Sealed records keep an adoptive person buried alive for his or her whole life," Fisher told *The New York Times* in 1982. "The outrage is that we must respect the rights of the adoptive parents and the birth parents. What about the rights of the adult adoptee being conditional on the whims of other people?"[9]

Clearly, adoptees were tired of being placated by people who insisted they knew what was best for them—and it's worth pointing out that this was true of a lot of people during those heady times. In the 1970s, daily headlines about the Watergate conspiracy, not to mention the multitude of deceptions behind the Vietnam War, destroyed years of collective trust in the wisdom of government authorities. Millions of Americans experienced, in a political sense, the adoptee's shock of discovery: They learned that the reality they had once accepted was, in fact, an ongoing deception.[10]

Adoption secrecy jangled other social nerves as well. Think of the popularity of the television miniseries *Roots*, a searing chronicle of American slavery, and of author Alex Haley's quest for personal identity. His story inspired millions of Americans, of all races and nationalities, to dig into their backstories. Genealogy became a major cultural pastime, sending millions into archives and churchyards in search of their great-great-great-great grandparents—and, ultimately, themselves. It was a popular movement from which adoptees were directly excluded, denied legal access to the most basic information about their origins, let alone the stories of their extended families.

Nor did it help that, during the post–Vietnam War years and then the Reagan era, international adoptions became entangled in some particularly nasty politics. What began as a humanitarian cause led by seasoned expatriates like Pearl Buck, an effort to make Americans reckon with the human toll of wars in China and Korea, began to look naive and arrogant—or worse, a misguided effort to cover the shame of the Vietnam debacle or vicious proxy wars in Central America. Against the background of ethnic pride movements in the 1970s and 1980s, celebrating the diversity and durability of immigrant cultures in the United States, adopting a Korean or Guatemalan or Chinese child seemed, at the very least, culturally insensitive. A privileged American life, critics charged, was hardly worth the pain of exile.

Then, of course, we need to consider the impact of feminism. Adoption had always been more a female than a male concern—it was about fertility and family after all, areas where society tended to give men a free pass or at least a minor role. But before the mid-twentieth century, adoption had never been a straightforward "women's issue" in the way we now define them. It had never pitted some women against others within the difficult realm of gender politics. That all changed with the rights revolution of the 1960s.

The shift began with our attitudes toward birth mothers. Once pitied or reviled, dismissed as fallen women or neurotic teenagers, they were now, under a feminist lens, emerging as real people. Gone was the old assumption that relinquishing a baby was the solution to an untimely pregnancy, or perhaps a just punishment for sexual immorality. Adoption was a cause of suffering, a primal loss that went far beyond the separation of mother and child in a hospital delivery room. One 1979 study of birth mothers used Elizabeth Kubler-Ross's stages of grief to describe their experience: Separation from an infant proved as painful as the actual death of a loved one.[11] Concerned United Birthparents, an organization formed in 1976, still exists to support all those damaged by the lifelong pain of adoption loss, the trauma of separation, and the exploitation of young mothers by a "billion dollar" adoption industry.[12]

Feminism also championed single mothers or at least enabled more women to support themselves and live independently. Between 1970 and 1980, the number of single parents in the United States almost doubled, increasing from 3.8 million to 6.9 million. Nearly all of them—some 90 percent—were women.[13]

Whether or not society lionized them depended on whether they were white or Black. On one side of the racial divide: Well-educated and well-employed white single mothers, like the fictional Murphy Brown, might be characterized as heroic, proof that feminine independence worked—and for the benefit of all. On the other side were Black single mothers, entangled in the backlash politics of welfare policy, a social problem no one wanted to solve.[14]

The right to privacy was also a tricky feminist issue. The movement had championed women's freedom to choose whether or not to carry a pregnancy to term, or in a larger sense, their fundamental right to manage their business without outside interference. But what about birth mothers? Did they have a right to privacy? Could they claim a right to freedom from prying eyes, especially if they had relinquished a child with the expectation that it was not, and would never become, public business?

By the 1990s, adoption had been caught up in a zero-sum language of legal rights. Here, the most dramatic instance was a ballot initiative in Oregon, known as Measure 58, which gave adoptees an absolute right to their original birth certificates, no exceptions. The move was led by Bastard Nation, a group out to challenge the old, often prudish attitudes surrounding adoption, and proud to reclaim "the badge of bastardy." "We see nothing shameful," their mission statement declares, "in having been born out of wedlock or in being adopted." A legal challenge from birth mothers claiming a right to privacy brought the issue to the US Supreme Court, which ruled against them. Measure 58 was a milestone for the search movement and the beginning of more and more openness in state laws, though the battles are still ongoing. What's most important about these legal cases, though, was the change in basic arguments about open adoption—now not just a matter of psychological health but a legal right to equal protection for adoptees. Closed adoptions, in other words, violate fundamental civil rights under the US Constitution.[15]

There were yet other complications, as, after the 1973 *Roe v. Wade* ruling, adoption became enmeshed in the polarizing cultural politics of abortion. For the pro-life movement, it was the obvious solution. Crisis Pregnancy Center provided women with logistical support—baby clothes and formula, a "shepherding home" with a Christian family—combined with stark, even lurid information about the mechanics of abortion. The New Right also took sides in the battles for open adoption, opposing any move to open adoptee birth records—standing against anything that might give a woman pause about bringing her child to term.[16]

Given the surrounding social turmoil, it's not hard to see why, even now, adoption makes people uncomfortable. It reminds us of uniquely troubled times in American history, our arrogant legacy of war and economic imperialism, our continuing exploitation of the poor and non-white. It makes us ask why the United States, alone in the developed world, does not seem to care about universal childcare or family leave. Worse, adoption doesn't sit neatly on either side of the present-day culture wars; it pits some women against other women, one race against another. It's all very confusing: On the one hand, we are a society built on at least the principle of equality, the idea that no one should be limited by their race, religion, sex, age, or disability. Yet, to quote Elizabeth Bartholet, who is both an adoptive mother and a professor at Harvard Law School, "Race and money: the longer you spend in the adoption world, the more you realize the power of these two factors" in determining who gets to be a parent.[17]

Finally, adoption evokes some dizzyingly difficult questions about individualism and identity, abandonment and trauma. It opens the troubling possibility that perhaps love is not enough in the face of pain and trauma. The adoptive parent's desire to love a child might in fact be a big part of the problem.

SCARY KIDS

Critics were not terrifically impressed when the movie *The Orphan* was released in 2009. A convoluted tale of an adorable yet homicidal Russian girl and her unsuspecting parents, the film was deemed "silly, overlong, and bloody as hell," according to *The Village Voice*. It was yet one more tired take of the "killer kid" genre. Yet even the big reveal at the end, that the "orphan" was actually a thirty-three-year-old woman with a pituitary disorder, did not deter audiences. In the end, the horror film did reasonably well, bringing in some $78 million.[18]

Pro-adoption groups attempted to protest, but with little effect. (Warner Brothers changed the voice-over on the movie trailer from "It must be difficult to love an adopted child as much as your own" to "I don't think Mommy likes me very much.") Clearly, old stereotypes lived on. Adoptees were secret psychopaths at best, little ticking time bombs of dysfunction ready to wreak havoc on their unsuspecting, naive adoptive parents.[19]

To make matters worse, a prequel was released in 2022, providing a gruesome backstory to the tale of the killer kid. We discover that the thirty-three-year-old orphan had already tricked another gullible family into taking her in, assuming the identity of their missing child. The plot unfolds with an array of improbable twists, this time involving everything from crossbows and arson to, yes, a dead-rat smoothie.[20]

A hundred years ago, an orphan was a sympathetic figure, admirable even. Readers loved characters like Little Orphan Annie and Tom Sawyer. Their resident adults—Daddy Warbucks and Aunt Polly—were also in the clear. Or at least they did not worry about being killed and dismembered by the children they had taken in. So why are we so threatened now? What exactly are we afraid of?

Blame the twentieth century, again. Our fears come courtesy of our therapeutic age, our extensive knowledge about personality development and our deep concern for personal identity. We are both endlessly curious about our inner lives and deeply fearful of the damage our minds might inflict upon us. We search for our true selves behind all the facades and falsity, and, all the time, we wonder whether there is anything worth finding.

Betty Jean Lifton deserves enormous credit for giving voice to the pain of many adoptees under the closed system and providing them with a powerful psychological argument. Like Fisher, she was a gifted writer who engaged in a long and difficult search for her birth parents and chronicled it in a best-selling book, *Twice Born: Memoirs of an Adopted Daughter*, published in 1975. Lifton followed it with two other important books, *Lost and Found: The Adoption Experience*, in 1979, and *Journey of the Adopted Self: A Quest for Wholeness*, in 1994.

The story she discovered about herself was painful and complicated—and inconclusive. Lifton's birth mother had gone on to marry and begin another family, and did not welcome a reminder, out of the blue, of an old and failed love affair. Not surprisingly, the relationship between biological mother and daughter was strained and sporadic. Nor was Lifton's birth father the man she might have imagined. He turned out to have been a bootlegger and self-described bon vivant, who had died shortly before a reunion would have been possible.[21]

Yet, in the end, all of the family-of-origin drama was beside the point. Lifton saw her story as an instructive parable, a rebuke to the secrecy and shame of closed adoptions and a warning about their psychologically traumatic effects on children. Moreover, there was considerable theoretical heft behind her argument: Not only was she a trained therapist, but her husband was Robert Jay Lifton, a leading authority on what we now call brainwashing. His work interviewing former POWs, veterans of the Korean War, helped establish a basic understanding of modern totalitarianism's psychological as well as physical brutality, its systematic manipulation of hearts and minds. Betty Jean Lifton's critique of adoption also built on theories about freedom and self-identity in books like Viktor Frankl's *Man's Search for Meaning*. Frankl's chronicle of survival in a Nazi prison camp emphasized the power of self-actualization, the basic human need for a sense of self and a chosen life purpose—a clear life story. "It came to me," she wrote, "that the way the adoption triangle is set up now, everyone in it is victimized. The whole system had to be opened up, restructured, if any one of the participants were to feel the inherent richness of its possibilities. Right now everyone at one time or another was dehumanized, limited, cheated, guilty."[22]

From there, the conversation around adoption became even more controversial. It was no accident, said Lifton, that the serial killer David Berkowitz was an adoptee and named himself Son of Sam. He was, after all, "a man who was not permitted to know whose son he was." Only the opening of adoption records would prevent future generations of adoptees from venting "their rage and frustration inward upon themselves," or "outward, like David Berkowitz on society."[23] In 1986, adoption was part of a legal defense argument for Patrick DeGelleke, who had killed his adoptive parents and burned down their house in a burst of psychotic rage. Lifton noted the young man's obsession with the phoenix, the mythological creature with the ability to rise up out of its own ashes. It seemed clear, she wrote in a *New York Times* editorial, that this mania had meaning: "The act of burning down his adoptive home was a metaphor for destroying his adoptive identity and resurrecting the heritage that had been taken from him." If his adoptive parents had understood that need, she said, perhaps they could have helped the troubled young man. "But they, like their son, were the victims of the denials inherent in the adoption system."[24]

The jury dissented, and DeGelleke was found guilty, but the idea of adopted child syndrome, a term first introduced in the DeGelleke trial, stuck. The idea that every adoptee is a potential serial killer seems outrageous, but Lifton was building on a body of psychological studies that have deeply influenced the way we see adoption. E. Wayne Carp, a historian who has traced this story in some detail, lays it at the feet of three extraordinarily prolific social scientists: Arthur Sorosky, a child psychiatrist at UCLA; Annette Baran, director of the Adolescent Treatment Program also at UCLA; and Reuben Pannor, the director of social work and research at the Vista Del Mar Child-Care Service in Los Angeles. Together, within the span of four brief years, from 1974 to 1978, these three published one book and eleven articles, an output that included not just your standard academic treatises but feature stories in big-circulation magazines like *Psychology Today*.[25]

Their influence was enormous. Carp credits these three researchers with changing the basic vocabulary of adoption, introducing terms that have become standard: the *adoption triangle*, for example, and *birth parents*, a change for the better from *natural parents*. They also challenged some basic assumptions. The old idea that a search for birth parents was a sign of neurotic maladjustment gave way to a new one, that searching was not only natural but necessary, possibly even mandatory. Otherwise adoptees were at risk for *genealogical bewilderment*, a loss of self-identity with all kinds of negative consequences, including self-destructive, even violent, behaviors.[26]

Carp, I should point out, has little use for these theories, dismissing them as "almost laughable in their empirical naiveté." His critique is unsparing, in fact, pointing out the regular use of heavily selective evidence or appallingly thin data. Sorosky, Baran, and Pannor did not apparently follow the normal protocols of their profession, certainly not considering the "mountains of data" that found adopted children doing just fine—that is, the 95 percent who did not end up in therapy. "From a social science methodological perspective," Carp writes, "it is a wonder that any of these articles were published."[27]

The problems with data and methodology in Sorosky, Baran, and Pannor's studies should not prevent us from acknowledging the very real pain that many adoptees experience, especially as adolescents. It's an unusually tricky time, clearly. We know that the rates of depression and attempted suicide among adoptees are nearly four times that of other adolescents. Without a doubt, being adopted can make the normal angst of those complicated years unspeakably painful. I know this. I have walked through a lot of this with my children, and, even now, I do not presume that our journey is finished.

That doesn't require going straight to tragedy though. Is it possible that adoptees suffer when we stigmatize adoption, when we worry, rightly or wrongly, that there must be something wrong with them? "Saying that adoption is a bad thing helps make it a bad thing," writes Bartholet. "In a world in which adoptive status is degraded, it will not feel good to be adopted."[28]

And we also know that times have changed. In the past several decades, interracial adoptions and those of older children have brought the old framework of secrecy down around itself. Not surprisingly, under the weight of social pressure and persistent lobbying, many state laws governing open and closed adoptions have liberalized, and it's fairly standard to allow adoptees full access to their records once they reach the age of eighteen. Many private agencies have also recognized the futility of holding the line on closure. Prospective parents could simply arrange a private placement with a birth mother and a lawyer. Even the popularity of DNA testing makes secrets almost impossible to keep—a 23andMe account could suddenly bring into your life not just a long-lost cousin but an entire array of relatives and a detailed extended family history.

In spite of all this progress, despite the fact that people have been raising other people's children for millennia, our wariness continues. Even when we know that the vast majority of adoptees apparently grow up into productive and happy adults—statistically only about 2 percent remain in therapy—we cannot escape the language of trauma.[29] In the popular imagination at least, biological ties are still the most real, the strongest—and also the safest.

LONELINESS

If, as I've pointed out, human beings have always taken in other people's children for the most part without worrying that the young ones were preparing for carnage, why are we so nervous about adoption today? I've offered many different explanations about why we are worried about the well-being of our priceless children, how our narrow definition of kinship and sense that biology is destiny have made the modern nuclear family our impossible ideal, how we have made motherhood such a precarious and painful task. Perhaps it's time to dig a little deeper, to turn the lens to our own psyches, to wonder if our fears of the stranger's child point to something more.

Perhaps the stranger's child has become a symbol, an uncomfortable reminder of what so many of us fear but are reluctant to name. It may well be that the real threat is not the orphan with violent tendencies but the modern problem of loneliness, the very real possibility many of us face that we may die alone.

Loneliness is now an "epidemic" in the United States. That's the stark word used very purposefully by former Surgeon General Vivek Murthy, who was concerned enough to write a book on the subject, one that ended up a best-seller. Murthy points out that, according to recent polling, one-quarter of all American adults—that's over 55 million people—experience some kind of harmful social isolation. Other surveys show that the number of adults living alone has doubled in the last fifty years; the number was up to 25 percent even before the pandemic, making it the highest rate ever recorded. And this trend is not rising just in the United States. A global survey conducted by Gallup in cooperation with Meta found similar proportions worldwide, and, most startlingly, the figure was highest among young adults, people roughly in their twenties.[30]

There's more and more evidence that chronic isolation is not just psychologically painful, it's physically debilitating. Separation from human support, an empty space where community should exist, literally saps the life from people. In fact, the health effects of loneliness are as bad as smoking fifteen cigarettes a day. Chronic isolation is more damaging to our bodies than obesity, excess alcohol consumption, or a sedentary lifestyle. Or to put it another way, people who do have strong and sustaining social ties are 50 percent less likely to die prematurely.[31]

Loneliness hurts, literally. The sensory fibers that register physical and emotional discomfort overlap in our brains. They travel down the same neural pathways. That's why it feels so bad to be ignored, why you flinch over a cutting remark, as if you'd been slapped. Solitude is bearable—in fact it can be a good thing: Just ask us introverts. A bit of quiet time in your own company can be delicious, even life-sustaining. But the enjoyment is possible because there is a prospect of return, a group of friends and family beyond the door of your monk's cell. When no one awaits, when there is no happy reunion in the offing, we suffer. We feel a hunger that goes down deep in our bodies, a need that goes back millennia, all the way back to our prehistoric ancestors. Like a sentient ape on a prehistoric savanna, we are afraid to be alone. We know that it is not good—it is not safe—to wander outside the community, beyond the possibility of help.[32]

These are big claims, of course, that need careful sorting through. Not everyone is affected by loneliness, and a good part of the problem is generational. In fact it's a particular affliction among younger people, contemplating their future in a world ridden with economic inequality and heading for climate disaster. These are the people, though, whose pessimism perhaps matters the most, making decisions about marriage and family in the midst of fundamental misgivings.[33]

Is it surprising, then, that adoption is nudging us in a vulnerable place? Projection is a powerful psychological tool, a way to lessen your personal discomfort by placing it on another, in this case on the stranger's child. That's not to say that concerns about trauma and separation are unfounded—adoption is not easy! The pain associated with it is real. But there may be more to our avoidance of adoption than we suspect, a story that is also about us.

We could begin by letting the adoptees off the hook, maybe liberate them from some stale preconceptions. There's no need, of course, to turn them into heroes, blessed by lucky stars, or, on the other hand, to brand them as victims, to see them as fundamentally damaged people. We can also recognize that a particular kind of wisdom comes with vulnerability, a sense of how the world works that's nuanced, ironic, and rare. Adoptees might have something important to say to us about belonging and bonding, fate and choice, what love means in a less-than-perfect world.

INVISIBLE PEOPLE

I know from my own family's experience that searches can be profoundly necessary and also very complicated. Anna's birth mother was not the person we had always imagined, based on the background information we received. She was not the plucky and determined teenager, the working-class

New Englander with curly brown hair and big blue eyes. The woman we met was a wry Southerner, a wounded refugee from poverty with a tragic past of deprivation and abuse. Finding her completed something for Anna—and for me. We had both wondered about her and hoped we would meet her. But meeting her also meant taking on family tragedies of people who were, and would remain, complete strangers.

Anna's birth father was a different story. He came to us courtesy of a genetic screening kit, in the form of an email from a biological cousin. We have only her birth father's picture, but it is enough. She is his image, right down to the shy but challenging gaze, the expressive tilt of the eyebrows. There are still so many mysteries, so much we don't know and can never know.

Adoptees are not the only ones living with unknowns, of course. Anna's story reminds me of my own genealogical bewilderment, my thin and episodic understanding of my own backstory. I cannot say much beyond my parents' generation, in fact. I had only a fleeting relationship with one of my grandparents—the rest had died before I was born—and he lived on the other side of the country, visiting us about once a year or so. I know almost nothing about the hardships and the hopes that brought that generation to the United States, nor do I know what it was like for them to be immigrants in a strange country. I have no clue about their lives as children, siblings, mothers, and fathers. Even my parents are somewhat of a mystery. Sifting through family papers, given to me after my father's death, I realize how little I knew him or my mom. Like many parents of bygone eras, their lives were lived apart from us, in private. Now, reading through my father's diaries and other family correspondence, I am coming across so much I never knew, so much I cannot fathom.

All families live with fictions. We have to: Anyone who tries to delve into the lives of their ancestors eventually comes up empty, asking questions that have no answers. Adoptive family relationships are constructed—in their case by law rather than biology—but in a larger sense, so are all family ties. They don't work automatically but require work, time, and attention.

We are all bewildered in some way, unable to make sense of the choices that other people made, long before we were born, that resulted in you or me. Even those of us who have researched family trees back to medieval times or have albums full of pictures of long-dead relatives are not entirely clear how those lives actually connect to us, how we came from them. We do not control as much as we'd like to think. We are all surrounded by invisible people. There are ghosts out there.

CHAPTER 7

GHOSTS

Some people compare adoption to a ghost story, and it's not hard to see why. Each member of the so-called adoption triad is accompanied by invisible others, specters floating just behind and beyond. For the birth mother, it might be the baby she relinquished, perhaps a lover she has lost, or the mother she might have been. The adoptive parents could be haunted by the child they never brought to life, a little one with their physical features, their personalities, and their family ancestry. And an adoptee might be contending with a multitude of spirits, not just ghostly birth parents and shadow siblings but the person they might have become *if*—if the adoption had never happened or if a different family had come to claim them, if different choices had been made. These are the ghosts of chance and contingency.

This metaphor makes sense to me, to a point. I do feel the others from time to time. They materialize when the extended family gathers, and the conversation is all about who looks like whom, who has whose nose and hair color. I listen, but I am distracted by an old and familiar chill up my spine. I feel a mysterious presence when I spot a random person with a striking resemblance to one of my children, an invisible other just beyond my sight. When we are celebrating a birthday, I sense that we are not alone.

True, some of the mystery has abated. We have changed the old laws designed to keep the spirits from manifesting, and adoptive families may now walk freely, without apology, in the clear light of day. The old shame has lifted; more people know their own stories.

But I don't think we've seen the last of the ghosts. They are notoriously indifferent to the concerns of the living. They pop in and out of our business without ever asking permission and then, just as quickly, vanish without explanation. You could say that the absence of manners is their defining characteristic. It's what makes them so unnerving: The very ones who could tell us what happens after death, answer all of our questions about heaven and hell, refuse to talk.

Way back when, ghosts had a lot to say. In Shakespearean plays and in daily life, supernatural beings often interrupted the lives of the living, warning them of danger or demanding justice for wrongdoing. For the most part, people took them at their word, assuming that a strange and startling visitation just had to speak truth. Somewhere in the past century, however, the ghosts stopped talking. Andrew Lang, a nineteenth-century British writer, declared the modern ghost essentially purposeless, a creature who "appears nobody knows why; he has no message to deliver, no secret crime to reveal, no appointment to keep, no treasure to disclose, no commissions to be executed, and, as an almost invariable rule, he does not speak, even if you speak to him."[1] Today's ghosts can be coaxed into séances or chased down hallways with night-vision cameras, but, for the most part, they are silent.

Despite the rebuffs, we continue to listen. A recent survey by a home security company found that half their clients believe their houses are haunted.[2] You could chalk this up to the new work rules: The more people work from home, the more they hear or think they hear. We also have a plethora of digital equipment, from phones to baby monitors, to capture uncanny moments—and post them online.

Some people have decided not to be afraid of their unearthly company. "I'm not opposed to a little bit of weird," a Wisconsin homeowner told a *New York Times* reporter in 2022. "The very first time I walked in the door," she said, "it felt like I was walking into a party that I wasn't invited to. It felt like everyone was looking at me, but I couldn't see them." Her biggest challenge was getting used to their odd sense of humor—the invisible companions would play little pranks, moving her shoes around or turning lights on and off. Over time, as all good roommates do, everyone learned to coexist. When people squabbled, one particularly irritable ghost would start slamming drawers in the kitchen.[3] Clearly, the dead enjoy their peace and quiet.

It seems that adoptive families are not the only ones haunted by ghosts. Everyone is haunted by something from their past, whether it's a broken friendship, a disappointed hope, or an unpursued opportunity. Every family is dogged by invisible fellow travelers, a host of might-have-beens and were-it-otherwises, the parents we wish we had had or wish we had been, the child who made a different set of choices, all the ancestors we will never know.

Mostly we treat these specters rudely. We ignore them, stuff them into closets, scream at them, order them out of the house. But what if we faced that fear and let them linger, maybe offered a bit of hospitality? Historian Erika Haysaki opens her book on transracial adoptions with a remarkable passage from the Vietnamese monk Thich Nhat Hanh: "If you look deeply into the palm of your hand, you will see your parents and all generations of your ancestors. All of them are alive in this moment. Each is present in your body. You are the continuation of each of these people."[4]

The deep truth of that statement offers us a way to ground ourselves and keep our imaginations alive. Love casts out fear, even fear of strangers—and their children. Adoption has been surrounded by worry, uncertainty, and risk. If we give in to those fears, we miss their gift, the way that stranger's child will unseat our pride, challenge our neat and tidy dreams, and fill with love places that we did not even know existed. We need those families, the messy and unpredictable, unfinished and inconclusive, adoptive and otherwise—people who do not, cannot, forget the many meanings of love, who never take them for granted.

ACKNOWLEDGMENTS

Many thanks are due to friends and colleagues who made this book possible. It came about as a conversation with my friends David Bratt and Laura Bardolph of BBH Literary, and, in the years since, they have coached and shepherded the manuscript with great patience and wisdom. I am very grateful for the support and astute advice of my editor at Beacon Press, Amy Caldwell, who has saved me from myself more than once.

I am also eternally grateful to Dana Robert and Daryl Ireland, my colleagues at Boston University's Center for Global Christianity and Mission, who, after my retirement, appointed me as a visiting scholar—and thus gave me full and miraculous access to the university library system and beyond, as well as opportunities to talk about this project with others in the program.

Most of all, of course, I am indebted to my husband Norman, who walked through all of this with me (and walks still), and the children I love more than I can ever say, Nate and Annie. We have all changed each other's lives, so many times and so much for the better. Blessings on you all.

NOTES

INTRODUCTION

1. National statistics about adoption in the US are surprisingly hard to track. The first census report on adoption was in 2000, and before that, the only national reporting was conducted by the US Children's Bureau between 1945 and 1975. Most of the information we do have has been collected by private agencies and advocacy groups. The statistical picture has also changed fairly rapidly due to the COVID pandemic, changing international law, and reforms in the foster care system. For recent statistics see Child Welfare Information Gateway, *Trends in U.S. Adoptions: 2010–2019*, U.S. Department of Health and Human Services, Administration for Children and Families, Children's Bureau, April 2022, https://www.childwelfare.gov/resources/trends-us-adoptions-2010-2019/; "Adoption Statistics," Adoption History Project, https://pages.uoregon.edu/adoption/topics/adoptionstatistics.htm; The Harris Poll, "2022 US Adoption Attitudes Survey," Dave Thomas Foundation for Adoption, February 2022, https://www.davethomasfoundation.org/resource/2022-u-s-adoption-and-foster-care-attitudes-survey/; Adoption Network, "US Adoption Statistics," https://adoptionnetwork.com/adoption-myths-facts/domestic-us-statistics/.

2. Bhavana Navuluri, "Adopted Child Syndrome: 7 Strategies to Prevent and Overcome It," *MomJunction*, last updated June 26, 2025, https://www.momjunction.com/articles/adopted-child-syndrome_00375730/. The condition is not listed in the American Psychiatric Association's *Diagnostic and Statistical Manual of Mental Disorders*, 5th ed. (2013), https://psycnet.apa.org/doi/10.1176/appi.books.9780890425596.

3. Kate Plummer, "Adoption Agencies Under Pressure 18 Months After *Roe v. Wade* Overturned," *Newsweek*, December 24, 2023,

https://www.newsweek.com/roe-wade-abortion-dobbs-adoption-1853724; Sydney Trent, "Women Denied Abortion Rarely Choose Adoption. That's Unlikely to Change," *Washington Post*, July 18, 2022; Elizabeth Kirk and Ryan Hanlon, "Why Most Americans Admire Adoption But Don't Choose It," Institute for Family Studies, July 15, 2025, https://ifstudies.org/blog/why-most-americans-admire-adoption-but-dont-choose-it.

4. Gabrielle Glaser, *American Baby: A Mother, a Child, and the Secret History of Adoption* (Penguin, 2021), 276. Also Larissa MacFarquhar, "The Fog," *New Yorker*, April 10, 2023, 32–49.

5. Fiona Bowie, "Adoption and the Circulation of Children: A Comparative Perspective," in *Cross-Cultural Approaches to Adoption*, ed. Fiona Bowie (Routledge, 2004), 4, 5.

6. Ellen Herman, "Child Adoption in a Therapeutic Culture," *Society* 39 (January/February 2002): 11.

7. Christine Ward Gailey, *Blue-Ribbon Babies and Labors of Love: Race, Class, and Gender in U.S. Adoption Practice* (University of Texas Press, 2010), 1–2; Danielle Taylor, "Fifteen Percent of Same-Sex Couples Have Children in Their Household," US Census Bureau, September 17, 2020, https://www.census.gov/library/stories/2020/09/fifteen-percent-of-same-sex-couples-have-children-in-their-household.html.

8. Gailey, *Blue-Ribbon Babies and Labors of Love*, 3.

9. Georgene Smith Goodin, "I Love My Children Enough to Wish I Had Never Met Them," *Boston Globe*, September 9, 2022, www.bostonglobe.com/2022/09/29/opinion/i-love-my-children.

10. Barbara Katz Rothman, *Weaving a Family: Untangling Race and Adoption* (Beacon Press, 2005), 7.

CHAPTER 1: CHILDLESS

1. Barbara Brown Taylor, *Learning to Walk in the Dark* (HarperCollins, 2014), 86.

2. Candida Moss and Jared Bader, *Reconceiving Infertility: Biblical Perspectives on Procreation and Childlessness* (Princeton University Press, 2015), 8.

3. Barbara Melosh, "Adoption Stories: Autobiographic Narrative and the Politics of Identity," in *Adoption in America: Historical Perspectives*, ed. E. Wayne Carp (University of Michigan Press, 2002), 222; Elaine Tyler May, *Barren in the Promised Land: Childless Americans and the Pursuit of Happiness* (Harvard University Press, 1995), 225.

4. Margaret Marsh and Wanda Ronner, *The Empty Cradle: Infertility in America from Colonial Times to the Present* (Johns Hopkins University Press, 1996), 14–15.

5. Nicholas Culpeper, *Culpeper's Directory for Midwives: or, A Guide for Women* (London, 1662), 132, 139.

6. John D'Emilio and Estelle B. Freedman, *Intimate Matters: A History of Sexuality in America*, 2nd ed. (University of Chicago Press, 1997), 183.

7. Quoted in Marsh and Ronner, *The Empty Cradle*, 45.

8. "A Mother's Love," *Ladies' Repository* 10, no. 1 (January 1850): 17.

9. Edward Clark, *Sex in Education, or, A Fair Chance for the Girls* (Houghton Mifflin, 1884), 70, 66.

10. C. G. Child, *Sterility and Conception* (New York: D. Appleton and Company, 1931); "Sterility and Neurotics," *Time*, June 16, 1952, 81–82.

11. Quoted in William H. Willimon, *Sinning Like a Christian: A New Look at the Seven Deadly Sins* (Abingdon Press, 2005), 51.

12. Scott Barry Kaufman, "The Opposite of Toxic Positivity," *The Atlantic*, August 18, 2021, https://www.theatlantic.com/family/archive/2021/08/tragic-optimism-opposite-toxic-positivity/619786/.

13. Thomas Merton, *Contemplative Prayer* (Doubleday, 1990), 24.

14. Nick Cave and Seán O'Hagan, *Faith, Hope and Carnage* (Farrar, Straus and Giroux, 2022), 159.

CHAPTER 2: CHILDREN

1. Janice Schroeder, "You Can Always Adopt," *Adoption and Culture* 10, no. 2 (2022): 221.

2. The story is told in Karen Ordahl Kupperman, *Pocahontas and the English Boys: Caught Between Cultures in Early Virginia* (New York University Press, 2019), 24–27.

3. *All's Well That Ends Well*, Act 4, Scene 5.

4. Ruth Wallis Herndon and John E. Murray, "'A Proper and Instructive Education': Raising Children in Pauper Apprenticeships," in *Children Bound to Labor: The Pauper Apprentice System in Early America*, ed. Ruth Wallis Herndon and John E. Murray (Cornell University Press, 2010), 8.

5. John Demos, *Past, Present, and Personal: The Family and the Life Course in American History* (Oxford University Press, 1986), 83–84.

6. Paula S. Fass, *The End of American Childhood: A History of Parenting from Life on the Frontier to the Managed Child* (Princeton University Press, 2016), 19.

7. *Memoir of Old Elizabeth, a Coloured Woman* (Collins, 1863), 3–4; Lester Alston, "Children as Chattel," in *Small Worlds: Children and Adolescents in America, 1850–1950*, ed. Elliott West and Paula Petrik (University Press of Kansas, 1992), 208–31.

8. Wilma King, *Stolen Childhood: Slave Youth in Nineteenth-Century America*, 2nd ed. (Indiana University Press, 2011), 233, 234.

9. Susan L. Porter, "A Good Home: Indenture and Adoption in Nineteenth-Century Orphanages," in *Adoption in America: Historical Perspectives*, ed. E. Wayne Carp (University of Michigan Press, 2002), 30; Linda Gordon, "Child Welfare: A Brief History," Social Welfare History Project, 2011, https://socialwelfare.library.vcu.edu/programs/child-welfare-overview/.

10. See, for example, Tim Hacsi, "From Indenture to Family Foster Care: A Brief History of Child Placing," *Child Welfare* 74 no. 1 (January/February 1995): 162–180; Marvin Olasky, "The Rise and Fall of American Orphanages," in *Rethinking Orphanages for the Twenty-First Century*, ed. Robert McKenzie (Sage Publications, 1998): 65–77.

11. Porter, "A Good Home," 31–32.

12. Catherine E. Rymph, *Raising Government Children: A History of Foster Care and the American Welfare State* (University of North Carolina Press, 2017), 21.

13. Fass, *The End of American Childhood*, 57.

14. The relevant details of this story are drawn from Lyle Dorsett, *Billy Sunday and the Redemption of Urban America* (Eerdmans, 1991), 9–13.

15. William T. Ellis, *"Billy" Sunday: The Man and His Message* (Philadelphia: John C. Winston Co., 1914), 25–26.

16. Dorsett, *Billy Sunday and the Redemption of Urban America*, 12.

17. Jeanne F. Cook, "A History of Placing-Out: The Orphan Trains," *Child Welfare* 74, no. 1 (January–February 1995): 185.

18. Cook, "A History of Placing-Out," 186.

19. Hacsi, "From Indenture to Family Foster Care," 67.

20. Brad Brooks, "Native Americans Decry Unmarked Graves, Untold History of Boarding Schools," Reuters, June 22, 2021, https://www.reuters.com/world/us/native-americans-decry-unmarked-graves-untold-history-boarding-schools-2021-06-22/.

21. Ellen Herman, *Kinship by Design: A History of Adoption in the Modern United States* (University of Chicago Press, 2008), 34.

22. Rickie Solinger, *Wake Up Little Susie: Single Pregnancy and Race Before* Roe v. Wade (Routledge, 1992), 49, 51–52, 52–53.

23. Rymph, *Raising Government Children,* 43–65; Linda Gordon, "Child Welfare: A Brief History," *Social Welfare History Project*, https://socialwelfare.library.vcu.edu/programs/child-welfare-overview/

24. Rymph, *Raising Government Children*, 2.

25. Children's Defense Fund, "Overview," *The State of America's Children, 2021*, https://www.childrensdefense.org/wp-content/uploads/2023/08/The-State-of-Americas-Children-2021.pdf.

26. Viviana A. Zelizer, *Pricing the Priceless Child: The Changing Social Value of Children* (Basic Books, 1985), 5.

27. Gloria L. Main, "Reflections on the Demand and Supply of Child Labor in Early America," in Herndon and Murray, *Children Bound to Labor*, 211; Felix Adler quoted in Zelizer, *Pricing the Priceless Child*, 6.

28. Zelizer, *Pricing the Priceless Child.*

29. Judith Warner, *Perfect Madness: Motherhood in the Age of Anxiety* (Riverhead, 2005), 196.

30. Warner, *Perfect Madness*, 192.

31. Fass, *The End of American Childhood*, 272.

32. Ariana Eunjung Cha, "10.5 Million Children Lost a Parent or Caregiver Because of COVID, Study Says," *Washington Post*, updated September 6, 2022, https://www.washingtonpost.com/health/2022/09/06/covid-deaths-orphans-worldwide/; Rhitu Chatterjee, "In a Decade of Drug Overdoses, More Than 320,000 American Children Lost a Parent," NPR, May 8, 2024, https://www.npr.org/sections/health-shots/2024/05/08/1249918051/drug-overdose-orphans-opioids-cdc-nida; Tim Requarth, "America's Pandemic Orphans Are Slipping Through the Cracks," *The Atlantic*, April 6, 2022; Joe Pinsker, "The Staggering Number of Kids Who Have Lost a Parent to COVID-19," *The Atlantic*, October 16, 2021.

33. Betty Jean Lifton, *Twice Born: Memoirs of an Adopted Daughter* (Penguin, 1977).

34. Nicole Chung, *All You Can Ever Know: A Memoir* (Catapult, 2018), 63.

35. Elizabeth Spiers, "I Have a Pretty Good Idea Why Michael Oher Is Angry," *New York Times*, August 26, 2023.

36. Nancy K. Gish, "Adoption, Identity, and Voice: Jackie Kay's Inventions of Self: Interview with Jackie Kay," in *Imagining Adoption: Essays on Literature and Culture*, ed. Marianne Novy (University of Michigan Press, 2004), 173.

CHAPTER 3: KIN

1. Susan Porter, "A Good Home: Indenture and Adoption in Nineteenth-Century Orphanages," in *Adoption in America: Historical Perspectives*, ed. E. Wayne Carp (University of Michigan Press, 2002), 33.

2. General Court of Massachusetts, "An Act to Provide for the Adoption of Children (1851)," in *Families by Law: An Adoption Reader*, ed. Naomi Cahn and Joan Heifetz Hollinger (New York University Press, 2004), 9–10.

3. "Our Adopted Baby," *Woman's Home Companion* 43 (April 1916): 5, 81.

4. Julie Berebitsky, *Like Our Very Own: Adoption and the Changing Culture of Motherhood, 1851–1950* (University Press of Kansas, 2000), 135.

5. Ellen Herman, *Kinship by Design: A History of Adoption in the Modern United States* (University of Chicago Press, 2008), 28.

6. Quoted in Herman, *Kinship by Design*, 39.

7. Rickie Solinger, *Wake Up Little Susie: Single Pregnancy and Race Before* Roe v. Wade (Routledge, 1992), 151; Herman, *Kinship by Design*, 32–39.

8. Herman, *Kinship by Design*, 1.

9. Child Welfare League of America, "Minimum Safeguards in Adoption," 1938, Child Welfare League of America Papers, Box 15, Folder 5, Social Welfare History Archives, University of Minnesota, accessed via https://pages.uoregon.edu/adoption/archive/CwlaMSA.htm.

10. Child Welfare League, https://pages.uoregon.edu/adoption/archive/CwlaMSA.htm.

11. Brian Paul Gill, "Adoption Agencies and the Search for the Ideal Family, 1918–1965," in Carp, *Adoption in America*, 161.

12. Herman, *Kinship by Design*, 111.

13. Herman, *Kinship by Design*, 70.

14. Quoted in Herman, *Kinship by Design*, 115.

15. Herman, *Kinship by Design*, 109; Ellen Herman, "Child Adoption in a Therapeutic Culture," *Society* 39 (January/February 2002): 13.

16. Gill, "Adoption Agencies and the Search for the Ideal Family," 172.

17. E. Wayne Carp, "Adoption and Disclosure of Family Information: A Historical Perspective," *Child Welfare* 74 (January–February 1995): 217–239; E. Wayne Carp, "The Sealed Adoption Records Controversy in Historical Perspective: The Case of the Children's Home Society of Washington, 1895–1988," *Journal of*

Sociology and Social Welfare 19, no. 2 (June 1992): 27–57. The ruse fell through in some cases in the 1940s, when young men enlisting in the military discovered they had no birth certificates.

18. E. Wayne Carp, "Introduction: A Historical Overview of American Adoption," in *Adoption in America: Historical Perspectives* (Ann Arbor: University of Michigan Press, 2002), 12–13; E. Wayne Carp and A. L. Guerrero, "World War II as a Watershed in the History of Adoption," in *Adoption in America: Historical Perspectives*, 181–217.

19. Quoted in Gabrielle Glaser, *American Baby: A Mother, a Child, and the Secret History of Adoption* (Penguin, 2021), 137.

20. Quoted in Solinger, *Wake Up Little Susie*, 93–94.

21. Glaser, *American Baby*, 1.

22. "Adoption Statistics by Race and Ethnicity in the U.S.," Legal Clarity, https://legalclarity.org/adoption-statistics-by-race-and-ethnicity-in-the-us/, April 1, 2026.

23. National Association of Black Social Workers, "Position Statement on Trans-Racial Adoption," September 1972, posted by the Adoption History Project, https://pages.uoregon.edu/adoption/archive/NabswTRA.htm.

24. Matthew Pratt Guterl, *Josephine Baker and the Rainbow Tribe* (Harvard University Press, 2014).

25. Pearl Buck, "I Am the Better Woman for Having My Two Black Children," *Today's Health* (January 1972): 21–22, 64; Soojin Chung, "How Missionaries Fostered World Friendship Through Transnational Adoption," in *Unlikely Friends: How God Uses Boundary-Crossing Friendships to Transform the World*, ed. David W. Scott, Daryl R. Ireland, Grace Y. May, and Casely B. Essamuah (Pickwick, 2021), 40–55.

26. Rhonda M. Roorda, *In Their Own Voices: Black Americans on Transracial Adoption* (Columbia University Press, 2015), 23, 144.

27. Roorda, *In Their Own Voices*, 4, 13.

28. Matthew Pratt Guterl, *Skinfolk: A Memoir* (Liveright, 2023), 291–92.

29. Janet Carsten, "The Substance of Kinship and the Heat of the Hearth: Feeding, Personhood, and Relatedness Among Malays in Pulau Langkawi," *American Ethnologist* 22, no. 2 (May 1995): 223, 234.

30. Nicholas Christakis, "In Some Cultures, Multiple Fathers—or No Fathers at All—Are the Norm," *Washington Post*, June 17, 2022.

31. Erdmute Alber, "'The Real Parents Are the Foster Parents': Social Parenthood Among the Baatombu in Northern Benin," in *Cross-Cultural Approaches to Adoption*, ed. Fiona Bowie (Routledge, 2004), 53–67.

32. Joseph Henrich, *The WEIRDest People in the World: How the West Became Psychologically Peculiar and Particularly Prosperous* (Farrar, Straus and Giroux, 2020), 33.

33. Henrich, *The WEIRDest People in the World*, 156, 157.

34. "The Future of Tribalism," *The Gray Area*, podcast with Sean Illing, June 22, 2023.

35. David Brooks, "The Nuclear Family Was a Mistake," *The Atlantic*, March 2020, https://www.theatlantic.com/magazine/archive/2020/03/the-nuclear-family-was-a-mistake/605536/.

36. *The Ascetical Homilies of Isaac the Syrian*, 81:51 as quoted in Paul Evdokimov, *The Struggle with God* (Paulist Press, 1966), 103, 216.

37. Charles Taylor, *The Ethics of Authenticity* (Harvard University Press, 1991), 29.

38. Tara Isabella Burton, *Self-Made: Creating Our Identities from Da Vinci to the Kardashians* (Public Affairs, 2023), 34, 233.

39. Janet Carsten, "Children in Between: Fostering and the Process of Kinship on Pulau Langkawi, Malaysia," *Man* 26 (September 1991): 428.

40. Charles Guignon, *On Being Authentic* (Routledge, 2004), 13.

CHAPTER 4: FATE

1. Edwin Chen, "Twins Reared Apart: A Living Lab," *New York Times*, December 9, 1979.

2. Chen, "Twins Reared Apart."

3. François Jacob, *The Logic of Life: A History of Heredity*, trans. Betty E. Spillmann (Pantheon, 1973), 19, 20.

4. Carl Zimmer, *She Has Her Mother's Laugh: The Powers, Perversions, and Potential of Heredity* (Dutton, 2018), 255.

5. Matthew Cobb, "Heredity Before Genetics: A History," *Nature Reviews Genetics* 7, no. 12 (2006): 957.

6. Francis Galton, "A Theory of Heredity," *The Journal of the Anthropological Institute of Great Britain and Ireland* 5 (1876): 331, https://doi.org/10.2307/2840896. Quoted in Staffan Muller-Wille and Hans-Jorg Rheinberger, "Heredity—The Formation of an Epistemic Space," in *Heredity Produced: At the Crossroads of Biology, Politics and Culture, 1500–1870*, eds. Staffan Muller-Wille and Hans-Jorg Rheinberger (MIT Press, 2007), 6;

Matthew Cobb, "An Amazing Ten Years: The Discovery of Egg and Sperm in the 17th Century," *Reproduction in Domestic Animals* 47 (August 2012): 2–6.

7. Henry Herbert Goddard, *The Kallikak Family: A Study in the Heredity of Feeble-Mindedness* (Macmillan, 1913).

8. Goddard, *The Kallikak Family.*

9. See discussion of the Kallikaks in Zimmer, *She Has Her Mother's Laugh,* 96–101.

10. Zimmer, *She Has Her Mother's Laugh*, 96–101.

11. From Goddard, *The Kallikak Family*, quoted in Russell Bonduriansky and Troy Day, *Extended Heredity: A New Understanding of Inheritance and Evolution* (Princeton University Press, 2018), 32.

12. Margaret Cobb, "The Mentality of Dependent Children," 1912, posted by the Adoption History Project, https://pages.uoregon.edu/adoption/studies/CobbMDC.htm.

13. Cobb, "The Mentality of Dependent Children."

14. Bruce Sacerdote, "How Large Are the Effects from Changes in Family Environment? A Study of Korean American Adoptees," *Quarterly Journal of Economics* 122, no. 1 (February 2007): 144.

15. Zimmer, *She Has Her Mother's Laugh*, 188–89.

16. Bonduriansky and Day, *Extended Heredity*, 4; Tori DeAngelis, "The Legacy of Trauma," *Monitor on Psychology* 50, no. 2 (February 2019), https://www.apa.org/monitor/2019/02/legacy-trauma.

17. Martha Henriques, "Can the Legacy of Trauma Be Passed Down the Generations?" BBC, March 26, 2019, https://www.bbc.com/future/article/20190326-what-is-epigenetics.

18. Bessel van der Kolk, *The Body Keeps the Score: Brain, Mind, and Body in the Healing of Trauma* (Penguin, 2015), 156.

19. Zimmer, *She Has Her Mother's Laugh*, 298–300.

20. Donna Liquori, "'The Chosen Baby': A Well-Loved Story," *Bibliofiles*, January 25, 2018.

21. Nicholas Christakis, "In Some Cultures, Multiple Fathers—or No Fathers at All—Are the Norm," Washington Post, June 17, 2022.

CHAPTER 5: MOTHERS AND OTHERS

1. Julie Berebitsky, *Like Our Very Own: Adoption and the Changing Culture of Motherhood, 1851–1950* (University of Kansas Press, 2000), 9, 76.

2. Jana Wolff, *Secret Thoughts of an Adoptive Mother* (Vista Communications, 2010), 109.

3. Laurel Thatcher Ulrich, *Good Wives: Image and Reality in the Lives of Women in Northern New England, 1650–1750* (Vintage, 1991), 157.

4. Ulrich, *Good Wives*, 157.

5. Samuel H. Preston and Michael R. Haines, *Fatal Years: Child Mortality in Late Nineteenth-Century America* (Princeton University Press, 1991), 3; Rebecca M. Cunningham, Maureen A. Walton, and Patrick M. Carter, "The Major Causes of Death in Children and Adolescents in the United States," *New England Journal of Medicine* 379, no. 25 (December 2018): 2468–75, https://www.nejm.org/doi/full/10.1056/NEJMsr1804754.

6. H. David Kirk, *Shared Fate: A Theory of Adoption and Mental Health* (The Free Press, 1964).

7. René A. Spitz and Katherine M. Wolf, *Grief, a Peril in Infancy*, The Researchproject, 1947, YouTube, posted October 7, 2019, by the National Library of Medicine, https://www.youtube.com/watch?v=LyVkXaqXOv4.

8. Virginia M. Schiller, *The Attachment Bond: Affectional Ties Across the Lifespan* (Lexington Books, 2017), 11.

9. Marshall D. Schechter, "Observations on Adopted Children," *Archives of General Psychiatry* 3, no. 1 (July 1960): 21, 9, 31, posted on The Adoption History Project, https://pages.uoregon.edu/adoption/archive/SchechterOAC.htm.

10. Heidi Keller, "Attachment Theory: Fact or Fancy?" in *Attachment: The Fundamental Questions*, ed. Ross A. Thompson, Jeffrey A. Simpson, and Lisa J. Berlin (Guilford Press, 2021), 233.

11. Gilda Morelli and Linxi Lu, "Pluralities and Commonalities in Children's Relationships: Care of Efe Forager Infants as a Case Study," in *Attachment: The Fundamental Questions*, ed. Ross A. Thompson, Jeffrey A. Simpson, and Lisa J. Berlin (Guilford Press, 2021), 240, 241.

12. Priscilla Witte, *There Are Moms Way Worse Than You: Irrefutable Proof That You Are Indeed a Fantastic Parent* (Workman Publishing, 2002).

13. Sarah Blaffer Hrdy, *Mother Nature: Maternal Instincts and How They Shape the Human Species* (Ballantine Books, 1999), 157–158.

14. Hrdy, *Mother Nature*, 151.

15. Chelsea Conaboy, *Mother Brain: How Neuroscience Is Rewriting the Story of Parenthood* (Henry Holt, 2022), 67.

16. Hrdy, *Mother Nature*, 157–158.

17. Hrdy, *Mother Nature*, 158.

18. Hrdy, *Mother Nature*, 115–16, 159, 538.

19. Conaboy, *Mother Brain*, 17–18, 116.
20. Conaboy, *Mother Brain*, 169.
21. Simone Weil, *First and Last Notebooks*, trans. Richard Rees (Oxford University Press, 1970), 71, 423; Simone Weil, *Waiting for God*, trans. Emma Craufurd (Harper, 2009).
22. Robert Zaretsky, *The Subversive Simone Weil: A Life in Five Ideas* (University of Chicago Press, 2021), 45.
23. Zaretsky, *The Subversive Simone Weil*, 52–54.
24. The term is from Ralph Waldo Emerson, as quoted in Tess Lewis, "Margaret Fuller: The American Mind Writ Large," *American Scholar* 65 (Spring 1996): 285.
25. Robertson Davies, *Fifth Business* (Penguin, 1977), 169, 21–22.

CHAPTER 6: SEPARATING

1. Nicole Chung, *A Living Remedy: A Memoir* (Ecco, 2023), 103, 106.
2. Chung, *A Living Remedy*, 18.
3. Mary Cardaras, "Adoption: Not a Default Setting," *Adoption and Culture* 10, no. 2 (2022): 199.
4. Quoted in E. Wayne Carp, *Family Matters: Secrecy and Disclosure in the History of Adoption* (Harvard University Press, 1998), 228.
5. Gina E. Miranda Samuels, "Epistemic Trauma and Transracial Adoption: Author(*iz*)ing Folkways of Knowledge and Healing," *Child Abuse and Neglect* 130 (2022), https://doi.org/10.1016/j.chiabu.2022.105588.
6. Grace Newton, "The Trauma and Healing of Consciousness," *Child Abuse and Neglect* 130 (2022), https://doi.org/10.1016/j.chiabu.2022.105563; Dominic McSherry, Gina E. Miranda Samuels, and David Brodzinsky, "An Introduction to the Adoption and Trauma Special Issue," *Child Abuse and Neglect* 130 part 2, (August 2022): 2, https://doi.org/10.1016/j.chiabu.2022.105691.
7. Rhonda Roorda, *In Their Own Voices: Black Americans on Transracial Adoption* (Columbia University Press, 2015), 104.
8. Carp, *Family Matters*, 41.
9. Sandra Gardner, "Adoption: Should Records Be Opened?" *New York Times*, June 13, 1982, https://www.nytimes.com/1982/06/13/nyregion/adoption-should-records-be-opened.html.
10. Carp, *Family Matters*, 146.
11. Carp, *Family Matters*, 207.
12. See Concerned United Birth Parents, https://concernedunitedbirthparents.org/, accessed January 16, 2026.

13. Steve W. Rawlings and Arlene Saluter, *Household and Family Characteristics, March 1994*, United States Department of Commerce, Bureau of the Census, 1995, xii–xvi.

14. Rickie Solinger, *Wake Up Little Susie: Single Pregnancy and Race Before* Roe v. Wade (Routledge, 1992), 223.

15. "Oregon Ballot Measure 58, 1998," posted by the Adoption History Project, https://pages.uoregon.edu/adoption/archive/BallotMeasure58.htm; Bastard Nation, the Adoptee Rights Organization, www.bastards.org/.

16. See, for example, Cullen Rogers-Gates, "The Gospel Centered Ministry of Adoption and Foster Care," under the auspices of the National Association of Evangelicals, https://www.nae.org/gospel-centered-ministry-adoption-foster-care/#.

17. Elizabeth Bartholet, *Family Bonds: Adoption and the Politics of Parenting* (Houghton Mifflin Harcourt, 1993), xvi.

18. Chuck Wilson, "Orphan: A Decidedly Amoral Thriller," *Village Voice*, July 22, 2009, https://www.villagevoice.com/2009/07/22/orphan-a-decidedly-amoral-thriller/.

19. David Crary, "Advocates of Adoption Upset by 'Orphan' Film," *Los Angeles Times*, July 19, 2009, https://www.latimes.com/archives/la-xpm-2009-jul-19-adna-orphan-movie19-story.html

20. Brian Tallerico, "Orphan: First Kill," RogerEbert.com, August 19, 2022, https://www.rogerebert.com/reviews/orphan-first-kill-movie-review-2022.

21. The story is told in her memoir, Betty Jean Lifton, *Twice Born: Memoirs of an Adopted Daughter* (Penguin, 1977).

22. Lifton, *Twice Born*, 247.

23. Betty Jean Lifton, *Lost and Found: The Adoption Experience* (Dial Press, 1979), 11. See also the discussion in Carp, *Family Matters*, 163.

24. Betty Jean Lifton, "How the Adoption System Ignites a Fire," *New York Times*, March 1, 1986.

25. Carp, *Family Matters,* 147–160.

26. Carp, *Family Matters*, 151.

27. Carp, *Family Matters*, 154, 155.

28. Bartholet, *Family Bonds*, 167.

29. Roorda, *In Their Own Voices*, 4.

30. Vivek Murthy, *Together: The Healing Power of Human Connection in a Sometimes Lonely World* (Harper Wave, 2020), 10; Ellyn Maese, "Almost a Quarter of the World Feels Lonely," *Gallup Blog*, October 24, 2023, https://news.gallup.com/opinion/gallup/512618/almost-quarter-world-feels-lonely.aspx.

31. Alexander Sherer, "America the Lonely: Social Isolation, Public Health, and Right-Wing Populism," *Berkeley Political Review*, March 25, 2021, https://bpr.berkeley.edu/2021/03/25/america-the-lonely-social-isolation-public-health-and-right-wing-populism/.

32. Murthy, *Together*, 50.

33. Bobby Duffy, *The Generation Myth: Why When You're Born Matters Less Than You Think* (Basic Books, 2021), 86.

CHAPTER 7: GHOSTS

1. Quoted in Owen Davies, *The Haunted: A Social History of Ghosts* (Palgrave Macmillan, 2007), 8.

2. Anna Kodé, "How to Live with a Ghost," *New York Times*, October 26, 2022, https://www.nytimes.com/2022/10/26/realestate/haunted-house-paranormal-ghosts.html; Heather Rose Artushin, "Do You Believe in Ghosts?" *Psychology Today,* October 9, 2025, https://www.psychologytoday.com/us/blog/well-read/202510/do-you-believe-in-ghosts.

3. Kodé, "How to Live with a Ghost."

4. Quoted in Erika Hayasaki, *Somewhere Sisters: A Story of Adoption, Identity, and the Meaning of Family* (Algonquin Books, 2022).

INDEX